MIXED

MIXED

EXPLORING WHAT IT MEANS TO BE BLENDED IN AMERICA

JEANNE JONES

www.mascotbooks.com

Mixed: Exploring What It Means to Be Blended in America

For more information, please contact:
Mascot Books
620 Herndon Parkway, Suite 320
Herndon, VA 20170
info@mascotbooks.com

Library of Congress Control Number: 2020918230

CPSIA Code: PRV1220A
ISBN-13: 978-1-64543-630-0

Printed in the United States

To my mother, Marie "Micky" Murray, our angel,
the best little shortstop in Maywood, Illinois.

CONTENTS

INTRODUCTION

WHEN I SET OUT IN APRIL 2018 to tell the story of our family, seeking to educate on the history of racism in our country and the impact it continues to have on families like ours, the foreword I had written shared my hope of reaching a handful of people that would "read it with open minds and empathy in their hearts, enabling a step forward in improving race relations in our divided country." I could have never predicted that before editing was completed, a movement stronger than any I had experienced in my lifetime would unfold.

I believed in 2018 there would be limited interest in or receptiveness to this topic; blacks were continually and repeatedly experiencing social injustice that was being ignored and discounted, while racist behaviors and policies were being increasingly protected and categorized as "political." Case in point: the racially charged reaction to Colin Kaepernick's right to peacefully protest, and the subsequent silencing of the black players who make up 70 percent of NFL team rosters. As the wife of a black man and the mother of black and biracial children, experiences with racial inequities have come to the forefront in a very personal way, and it made my desire to move forward with the book more important than ever. I began to mentally prepare myself to be met with resistance by not just the obvious haters, but even by people I believed were friends. Based on the complicity I had repeatedly observed over the past couple of years and the lack of willingness to engage in and advocate for change, I expected to be met with the usual narrative: "People like me are making a big deal out of nothing." This is a position that has become increasingly popular with racists in America.

As I write this, it is with a less heavy heart than before; a heart that for the first time in years is beginning to believe that the voices that have been silenced for so long may now be beginning—albeit only beginning—to be heard. In the few short weeks since my final draft was submitted for editing, our country has been shaken and awoken by the senseless and racially motivated deaths of George Floyd and Ahmaud Arbery, and national protests were beginning on behalf of Breonna Taylor. We hit a tipping point, one that many have been waiting, and waiting, and waiting for.

Lights are coming on; the sun is rising on America and beginning to shine; locked doors are opening; the fog is lifting; the rose-colored glasses are coming off. It is imperative we do not dim the lights because the truth is blinding. Rather, we must listen intently, with eyes wide open, and fight to be a country that emulates the vision that was established centuries ago but has never become a reality—a land where all people are created equal.

"Change will not come if we wait for some other person or some other time. We are the ones we've been waiting for. We are the change that we seek."

—*Barack Obama*

Jeanne Jones

CHAPTER 1
MEET THE JONESES

ONE MORNING IN FEBRUARY 2018, my biracial son, Quincy, woke up in his dorm room at the University of Nebraska–Lincoln (UNL) and learned his university had made national news overnight. His biracial roommate and childhood friend, Austin, showed him a video that had been circulating on Twitter that morning about a fellow student who claimed to be "the most active white nationalist in the Nebraska area." The video was shared by Anti-fascist Action Nebraska to demand the university take action. UNL tweeted that they were taking the matter "very seriously," but they made no other comments.

Quincy watched the video on his way to class. In the video, Anti-fascist Action Nebraska had included clips of the student in question looking right at the camera during a recorded Google Hangout session with other white nationalists. He looked a lot like several other students on campus—fluffed hair and wearing a blue T-shirt. There was a bowling ball in the background of his dorm room.

"Just because I dress like a normie—a presentable person—doesn't mean that I don't love violence," he said. "Trust me. I want to be violent. Trust me. Really violent," he continued.

"You don't have to look like a violent person to be violent." And this student *had* been violent. The video showed the student at the Unite the Right Rally in Charlottesville, Virginia, the year before, participating in violent acts with the group Vanguard America. In the Hangout, he said about those who threatened his life after the rally: "They haven't done anything because I obviously walk around campus all day with a smile on my face." Quincy was suddenly very aware of the color of his skin. This student could be anywhere on campus, around any corner, hating someone he hasn't even met, just because that someone has the audacity to exist.

✳ ✳ ✳

Later that afternoon, Quincy walked into his African American history class. He took a seat as his professor started talking. "There's a video going around campus," the professor began.

Quincy had initially enrolled in the class to find out more about his heritage and to connect with a black professor. Ironically, his African American history professor was white.

The professor, running his hands through his blond hair, got the class up to speed. Once he was finished explaining the contents of the video, he stood up quickly. "Gather your things," he said. "We're going to the Multicultural Center to meet with the chancellor and the police department." The fifteen or twenty students in the class grabbed their backpacks and headed out of the classroom.

The meeting was already about twenty-five minutes in by the time Quincy's class arrived. Fifteen or twenty students—mostly grad students—were already peppering questions at the men and women up front. White students cried outrage and pulled up the student handbook to cite acceptable reasons for expulsion. Black students spoke about feeling unsafe at school. UNL is less than 3 percent black; they already felt like outsiders, and this video made them feel even more so. But the true icing on the cake was that the authorities didn't reprimand this student at all. "He didn't start a riot on campus," they said. "He didn't do anything that goes against University policy."

Quincy called me as he left the meeting. He normally only texts, so when I saw his number on my phone I felt my heart rate pick up as the all-too-common what-if scenarios came racing in—scenarios that had frequented my mind since the first day I dropped him off at UNL.

"Mom?" he said. I immediately sensed the urgency in his voice. I held my breath and listened intently as he struggled to describe what he had just been through. The words were difficult to come by, but I know my son, and I could easily translate his brief overview of the experience into the frustration, rage, and confusion boiling inside him. *What the hell was happening?* At that moment, our lives changed. Everything I'd taught him about American progress seemed to be a lie. He felt deflated, scared, and vulnerable—all emotions I had, through hard work, raised him to reject or overcome. He said public colleges were supposed to be progressive, even ones in the Midwest. He said he didn't belong. How could I encourage him otherwise, when my reaction was to want him out of there?

This was the day the aching voice in my head—the one that kept hinting that things were getting worse—became a very loud and clear *outside* voice. It was an undeniable, factual confirmation that reprehensible actions and words, which leaders would have quickly condemned and quieted just years ago—even if motivated by being politically correct and not authentic—were now being protected. With this outside voice came the realization that my younger children would be up against an even greater battle than I had ever imagined.

In one of his videos, this same student proclaimed the Founding Fathers didn't care about the opinions of Mexican Americans or African Americans. The college sure didn't seem to, and the administration adamantly refused to expel him, citing the First Amendment as justification for taking no action. In a *Newsweek* article dated February 13, 2018, a spokesperson for the school responded, "The University of Nebraska can't discriminate against someone for having unpopular political beliefs." *Political beliefs? Really?* My son was attending the largest university in the state of Nebraska, which we learned that day happens to believe that racist, violent threats are considered "political beliefs." I did not realize then how the reverberations of this statement would continue to unfold over the following two years.

In a show of solidarity, the UNL basketball team considered boycotting their Saturday game. But in the end, they showed up wearing shirts with the words "Hate Will Never Win" printed across the front. The coach, Tim Miles, fully supported them. It was one bright moment of courage and decency at the end of a horrible week.

✳ ✳ ✳

My husband, Keith, and I live in Omaha, Nebraska, with our ten-year-old biracial twin girls, Ezley and Xonya. My stepson,

Kaydon, who is black and of course an equal member of our family, is fifteen years old and stays with us part time. Quincy, now twenty-one years old, left UNL after his freshman year and attends the slightly more diverse University of Nebraska Omaha and rents his own apartment. It's with pride and a mother's natural trepidation that I watch his independent, young adult story as a black man in America unfold.

Keith and I were fortunate to have met each other later in life, and we never would have expected our lives to evolve—and connect—in the ways they have. We were both raised in poor, religious households with six other siblings. We were both in serious relationships that ended in infidelity (two marriages for him and a marriage and long-term relationship for me), and we both left Omaha to pursue careers, then found ourselves back in our hometown where we met for the first time.

Ours is the American story. Our daughters Ezley and Xonya can trace their lineage back to the Revolutionary War on one side of the family and to the slave trade on the other—a dichotomy at its finest. My father's ancestor Timothy Knox, who served in the Revolutionary War, founded Woodstock, Vermont, while in exile. My mother's family came to the United States from Czechoslovakia via Ellis Island on the ship *Valparaiso*. My ancestors changed their names to sound American, which was a common practice for immigrants at the time. One of Keith's ancestors, Lorenzo Hughes, was a runaway slave from Virginia who was caught and sold to a family in Mississippi that gave him, and future generations of his family, their surname. After the Civil War, Lorenzo became a sharecropper for a wealthy black man named Home Teel. It was rare to have the opportunity to sharecrop for a black man. That sharecropper's progeny would one day include a humble running back for the NFL, my husband Keith Jones, nicknamed End Zone Jones.

My parents, Lawrence and Marie, married when my mom was a twenty-nine-year-old virgin. By the age of thirty-seven, she had delivered all seven of us kids. Three of us are not even a full year apart. She had wanted twelve kids. I was the second youngest and was born in 1969. Before he met my mom, my father, who was interested in becoming a Roman Catholic priest, took a vow of poverty, and that didn't change as our family grew. He was offered high-paying jobs because he could do computer programming before computers were mainstream, but he turned them down. He is a certified genius and an early member of Mensa, but he held onto poverty almost like it was his own personal martyrdom.

We lived in a one-story, ranch-style home with three bedrooms and one bathroom. We also had a partially finished basement that we cherished. Some of us slept in the living room on fold-out couches. I slept on a beanbag until third grade. I remember my parents saying in the mornings, "Don't forget to make the couches!" We went to schools where the majority of students were middle class, and many were upper-middle class. We were definitely an exception, living below the poverty line. But we had pride in what we did have.

Our neighbors, the Chavezes, whose father Victor is of Iberian and Native American decent, also had six children—three boys and three girls—following closely in line with our family. Vic would set up shop in our kitchen and cut my dad and brothers' hair. As a child it was fun to hear his accent and have early exposure to a second language; it was not something our elementary school offered. We appreciated that their family was "like us." When our classmates asked about why we were getting free lunches at school, we could say "because we both have so many kids in our families." Kelly Chavez was just a year younger than me and would grow to be one of my best friends, standing by my side through some of the most challenging times of my life.

My dad worked for Boys Town (also called Father Flanagan's Boys' Home) for over fifty years as a counselor and then in administrative roles. It was there, on the Boys Town campus, that I made friends with people who came from the most difficult and adverse circumstances—friends who made my humble but stable home life seem grand. Unlike many of our classmates, while at Boys Town we were surrounded by people who didn't look like us, people from whom we would learn important life lessons. I had no idea then that decades later I would be so grateful to have that intentional, critical exposure to diversity that my father encouraged.

Most of us siblings lived in the basement. We loved this cold, small (but more private) space. The windows weren't fully sealed, so bugs and critters got through, and snakes sometimes came out of the drain. We were thrilled when Boys Town gave us a couple of donated beds. Two older siblings got their own rooms. The downstairs area felt like our own little home. In our teenage years, we had a small TV with a rabbit ear antenna that sometimes worked; a few years later, we got our own phone that hung on the wall. There were particle board walls and two doors creating two bedrooms in the basement. Three of my sisters and I shared the open space at the bottom of the stairs where we kept a freezer stocked with loaves and loaves of bread from the thrift store. We used the freezer as a makeshift dresser, sometimes stacking our clothes in neat piles on top, other times throwing them there haphazardly. My oldest brother had one of the basement rooms, and my oldest sister had the other. This arrangement became the source of taunting from a classmate, who liked to comment that "she lives in a basement and shares a room with her brother." Although it hurt at the time, I have grown to really understand the ignorance of this comment and feel sorry for this girl; what a small and comfortable world indeed she must have lived in to find siblings sharing bedrooms uncommon or disturbing.

After my brother moved out and went to college, my sister and I got to move into that room, and we got our own "closet"—a vinyl accordion-style hanging door. We felt so lucky because it was *ours*. It wasn't until I turned twenty-seven that I purchased a dresser that I would call my own. There simply had not seemed to be a need for one after being accustomed to using crates and stacking my clothes.

My dad refused to take pay raises for years, until Father Peter pointed out that to not provide them was illegal, or at best against Boys Town's policy. My mom was extremely resilient, but she sometimes got upset about our financial situation. I remember her lying on the bed with her checkbook, saying silent prayers that the checks she had written would not clear before the next paycheck came. We'd go to the grocery store, and she would quietly, and shamefully, tell us to put this and that back. Unless you have experienced it, it is difficult to describe how deep those emotions can run, and the lasting impact they can have on one's psyche. I imagine the feelings are just as real for those born into wealth and trying to prove themselves. I always try to maintain an open mind and not judge others for what they have been given and not earned for that reason, just as I didn't want others to judge me for what I didn't have. I believe this is also what has driven me to constantly pursue a greater understanding of the experience of underserved communities.

After I graduated high school and my parents didn't have the expense that came with caring for all of us, my mom shared with me how conflicted she had been about not being able to give us "things" other kids had. I assured her we were surrounded by love, and we knew how fortunate we were. Every year, Christmas was magical. Our mom went to great lengths to ensure she spent the exact same amount of money on each of us, even though there was little to go around, and she made sure every sibling had the same number of presents. She cased garage sales throughout the year and would go so far as giving one of us a kitchen utensil to make the present count even.

For several years during the summers and on holidays, my family welcomed five college basketball players from Panama, Puerto Rico, and the Dominican Republic to stay in our home. They ranged from 6′ 6″ to 6′10″. One of our guests—my brother's roommate—was leading the nation in scoring for NCAA Division II basketball. Despite our already cramped living space, we always had room. They taught me to appreciate what we had. They couldn't go back home to see their families, so we tried our best to fill that gap.

They were protective of my sisters and me and taught me to speak Spanish. But most importantly, they taught me about their cultures and opened my eyes to the privilege I was born into and the responsibility I had to speak up for those who were not born into that privilege. The small school they played for in Iowa lacked diversity, and they played schools with similar diversity issues. I had to watch from the stands as the opposing teams threw bananas and chanted things like, "Go back to Panama." The opposing teams played "Born in the U.S.A." and waved an American flag at individuals who had grown to become my brothers. My dad wrote letters in protest to those schools; we made sure to swarm our players after the games, letting them know they were welcomed and loved and didn't deserve the racist treatment from those other teams.

Keith's mother and father were both sharecroppers. Keith was born in North Omaha (the birthplace of Malcolm X) in 1966, shortly after his mother and father moved from Mississippi to establish a better life by working in one of the meat production plants. He was raised in a two-bedroom home as the youngest of seven children. He recently discovered he has a younger half-brother named Maurice. Keith was about four when his parents separated, and his dad moved out of state. His mom was pretty much left to raise the seven of them alone, and she did so for years. His dad came back maybe once a year. Even though it was so infrequent, he was their father, so it was exciting for them whenever he showed up. Keith has told me that when you're a kid, you don't realize the disconnect between what your father does and what he *should* do—especially compared to your mother—when he isn't around. His appreciation for his mother now runs deep, to say the least.

Keith watched all his older siblings go through different challenges, and as the youngest child, he learned a lot from observing the outcomes of the various choices they made. He knew if he wanted to avoid any unfavorable outcomes, he had to make the opposite choice from a sibling who'd made a bad one. This is a benefit the younger siblings almost always have.

He and his brothers got involved in sports at a young age in order to have something positive to do with their time. After first playing baseball and wrestling, Keith watched and then joined an organized football team in his neighborhood; he realized quickly the sport came naturally to him—even during his very first drill when he, playing running back, kept outrunning the coach, who acted as the linebacker. He got tired of the coach calling him names for continuously getting past him and decided one day to simply walk off the field and head straight home. Other coaches had already heard about his potential, and one was quick to offer him a spot on their team. At that young age, Keith was able to sense authenticity in adults, or the lack thereof, and he had the courage and intuition to respond in a way that was mature beyond his years.

Keith says sports kept him occupied, focused, and busy. He started running track, and while it didn't come as easily as football, his desire to improve and constantly pursue a personal best led him to become faster and faster with practice. Since Keith's dad wasn't around, the coaches, both in track and football, served as male role models for him, as did his Uncle Steve. It became clear to him that success wouldn't come without discipline and work ethic.

Keith attended one of the most racially diverse high schools in Omaha—Central High. During this time, he kept playing football and running track, and he started seeing success in both sports. A lot of it had to do with ability, but he adamantly believes the work ethic was more important. He learned to not expect a payoff unless he put in the time and effort. If someone was faster than him, he knew he had to work harder. With football there were running backs who were better, so he put the work in to beat them. By the end of his senior football season, he had broken the school's all-time rushing record that had been set by the great Gayle Sayers. The direct correlation between the level of effort and reward continued to be validated throughout his life, and he especially kept that mentality throughout his football career.

As for me, I started working full time when I was sixteen years old. I didn't have much of a life outside of work and school. I didn't have your normal experiences with dating in high school, because I was very restricted with where I was allowed to hang out. One exception was going to the Boys Town field house, and there was always supervision there. My days started at 5:30 a.m. with cheer practice, student council during final period, then off to work from 4:00 p.m. until 11:00 p.m. or later, with full workdays on the weekends. I also managed to fit in babysitting hours, and the summer after graduating I worked three jobs to save for college. That nose-to-the-grindstone outlook is something Keith and I share, and it bonded us from the beginning.

I started supervising a team of about twenty when I was just eighteen years old. It was tough. Many of the employees were in the workforce full time, and telemarketing was their second job; I was the one who had to coach them on their call handling and closing skills. At the time, telemarketing was relatively new, and Ameritech had just started in the cell phone business. The cellular division was recruiting someone with call center experience, and they happened to be outsourcing their contact center to the company I had worked for. My now ex-husband got recruited first and moved to Chicago. I was still living in Omaha, and Ameritech said they needed a call center manager. I was twenty-six years old when they brought me on. By the time

I was twenty-seven years old, they promoted me. At this young age, I was an assistant director at a Fortune 500 company, with stock options and a 401(k). My boss was telling me he had a plan for me and that I was going places. I embarked on my master's degree full time, while pregnant with Quincy and working full time in a round-the-clock call center carrying a pager.

Things quickly shifted for me as my life seemed to enter a downward spiral. In addition to my mother having a heart attack and going through open heart surgery, my marriage to Quincy's dad rapidly deteriorated shortly after Q was born. I felt guilty for getting divorced, but I knew Quincy needed stability in his life more than he needed the promise of siblings, which I desperately wanted to give him, having been one of seven children. During the marriage, I had relocated with my ex to Chicago and then to Kansas City, living with his mother through this difficult time. But after the split, I made the tough decision to leave an amazing job and take a significant pay cut and demotion to permanently move back to Omaha so Q could be close to his cousins. This was the first big pay cut that I took in an effort to prioritize my family, but it wouldn't be my last.

Unfortunately, not too long after the divorce, I got into a toxic relationship that lasted four years. My mother was alive during this time and I could see the disappointment and sadness in her eyes when she would lovingly and nonjudgmentally ask me how things were going; she knew instinctively as a mother that I was not in a good place and was with a man who did not love me.

Since my mom's passing, I have talked to her frequently and been specific in asking for help. She witnessed the trials and tribulations I have been through, and I knew she wanted nothing more than for me to be in a healthy and loving relationship. I told her if I was going to be with someone, he would need to fit very specific criteria. He would have to be someone who could appreciate having moved away from Omaha to do other things; someone who had a big family; someone who wanted to be a part of my family; and someone who experienced firsthand what it's like to be a single parent. I had a list of characteristics a mile long that needed to be met if I was ever going to open up and trust again. It is not a coincidence that Keith met everything on that very detailed list—my mother had picked him for me.

In high school, Keith's brother, Lee, who was one year ahead of him, got a scholarship offer to play at the University of Nebraska–Lincoln. That's when Keith first realized he might have a shot. He thought, *If Lee can do it, I can too.*

Keith wasn't sure if he'd get a chance to play in the NFL. He was a running back, and most of the running backs he admired were big guys like Herschel Walker, Earl Campbell, and Bo Jackson. Some of them were over 6′ tall and over 200 pounds. Keith was 5′9″ and 180 pounds. He had a lot of naysayers telling him he was too small. Then a running back named Tony Dorset, who was similar in size to Keith, ended up being drafted to the Dallas Cowboys—one of Keith's favorite teams. When Keith saw what Tony was capable of, he thought maybe he could do it too. But he still wasn't sure.

It was during Keith's second year of college that he realized he might have a shot at going pro. Once a year, at just about every NCAA Division I school, the scouts came to evaluate players. His coach made sure Keith came to the evaluations, and he told the scouts that Keith was one of the few underclassmen that was going to run the 40-yard dash. On the first attempt, he was a mere hundredth of a second off from breaking the school record for football players. They scratched their heads and asked him to run it again. The second time, he ran a little faster. He looked over, and they were showing each other the stopwatch in amazement. He thought, *If these guys are impressed, maybe I do have a shot.* That 40-yard dash record of 4.33 seconds electronic (4.13 handheld) still holds at the university today, three and a half decades later.

After that, he just tried to get better. He continued to work hard and compete in games. He got little nicks and bruises, and he fought and overcame them. By his senior year, he was an all-conference player. Back then it was the Big Eight, and out of those eight schools, he was the leading rusher. Nationally, he was ranked eighth or ninth. He made Honorable Mention All-American and was lovingly referred to by college football fans across the nation as End Zone Jones.

Keith's transition from college to the professional level was pretty similar—the players were equal or better, and everyone was fighting for a job. But at the professional level, they're just looking for the all-around best players. The focus shifted to making a team, not about what position you played. Most of the guys weren't too excited about special teams on the professional level, but Keith was looking for an opportunity—special teams was just that.

Keith ended up getting drafted by the Los Angeles Rams, then went to the Cleveland Browns, then the next year to the Dallas Cowboys. Once he made it to the NFL, he knew what he needed to do to sustain himself and keep progressing. When he signed with the Cowboys, he felt like he was at the pinnacle of health. He had sustained a couple concussions, but back then those weren't considered injuries. With a couple years under his belt, he knew what the coaches expected and what he had to do during practices to meet those expectations.

The 1990 off-season training was rigorous, and shortly after training camp actually started, Keith injured his knee. Then, a domino effect of injuries took place. A knee injury as a running back is an uphill battle. He was confident enough in his work ethic that he thought he'd be okay and bounce back. But about six months into his rehab, he ruptured a disk in his spine. That set his rehab back for his knee, because now he had to rehab his back first.

Keith was rushed during rehab. His contract with the Cowboys was valuable, and he knew the NFL was a business and they needed to get their money's worth. Coach Jimmy Johnson had announced Keith on his local television show as the starting running back, despite having a very promising rookie named Emmitt Smith added to the roster. They wanted him to get back out on the field, but it was just physically impossible. Coach Johnson called him into his office and wanted to know why he wasn't "willing" to come out and practice.

Keith told him, "You know the deal. I just started my rehab a month ago, and I was delayed four months for my back. I'm not ready to practice yet."

"Well," Johnson said, "if you're not, we have to do what we have to do." He released Keith from the team.

After that meeting, Keith talked to his agent. They immediately filed a lawsuit. A few months later, they won an arbitration hearing. Because of the hearing, Keith got the extra year he needed for his pension. At the time, he didn't know what the future would bring and all that was riding on the arbitration. What he did know: it was time for End Zone Jones to turn the page. And his decision to not take on further physical risk was the right one; although his outward appearance is healthy, he is now permanently disabled from his injuries and experiences daily challenges that others his age take for granted.

Keith and I both had relationships where our exes took from us—financially and emotionally. We were both prey. People could sense our vulnerability, and they took advantage of it. Keith knew that next time around he wanted someone independent and self-motivated—someone who would see him as a partner and not a business investment.

Keith and I met in our thirties after both having lived in larger cities with more diversity. I had recently become friends with a single mom like me, Kris, who also happened to have a biracial son. One night early in our friendship, Kris invited me out to a local restaurant and lounge. She had a friend who was in town from Cleveland with some of his friends, and she asked me to join her. Her friend brought his brothers, Keith and Tony.

That night I did not meet Keith, but I spent time talking to his brother Tony. Ironically, I already knew him—he had played on a flag football team with my ex—so we spent some time catching up. In our conversation, I mentioned that I was looking for a new car, and he insisted I give his brother Keith a call, who was working for a dealership at the time. Later that week I did. We completely hit it off over the phone, talking for about forty-five minutes before we decided I would make an appointment to come in and look at cars.

Shortly after that phone conversation with Keith, Kris reached out to see if I wanted to get out for a while. Q was with his dad for the weekend, and since I was recently single, it was really great to be out and social again with someone I could really connect with. Tony had called Kris to ask where she was and what her plans were for the night; she suggested he meet us out. Keith would be with him.

They got there at about 10:00 p.m., after Keith got off work. I let him know I was the one who had called him about a new car, and we picked up the conversation right where we had left off. He bought me a drink, and unlike with my past and very limited experiences in the dating world, the conversation flowed easily. After a few drinks, I tearfully told Keith about how I didn't want Quincy to be an only child. Being newly single and in my thirties, this was emotionally weighing on me. I wanted Q to have brothers and sisters like I did. After I said it, I immediately reminded myself that such talk is "repellant" in the dating world, but I didn't care. I was planning to do this on my own, like I had everything else, and I shared my goal with him.

Keith barely hesitated before replying, "I would have a baby with you." It was coming from a place of empathy and understanding, and I did not take it literally. We both had shared that we had no intentions of ever being in a relationship or marrying again. It actually made sense. Quickly establishing this seemed to take the pressure off and allow us to focus on just getting to know each other as friends.

The friendship quickly evolved, and Keith asked me out to dinner. Our first date was to a small restaurant down the street from my house. The conversation flowed, but the food was awful. We were able to joke about it and roll with it. After the date, five days transpired and he still hadn't called to arrange another. I was raised not to pursue boys. They call you, not the other way around. I had a great time on our date, but I was beginning to think Keith felt differently, and that was fine with me. I wasn't searching, and I sure wasn't desperate; I had been independent and taking care of myself for years. Finally, he called.

"I didn't think you were going to call me again," I said.

"Well, you never called me," he responded.

"Why would I call you? I don't chase men," I explained.

"Uhhh… I've never had to call," he said. "Women have always called me."

"Just know, I'm not going to be calling you. I'm not going to chase you," I said. I knew it sounded old-fashioned, but I felt it was important to send a message about my newly cherished self-worth. He ended up liking that about me—it wasn't something he was used to.

When I had been talking to Keith's brother Tony, he had shared that Keith had played football for Nebraska. I didn't think much of it because many former Nebraska players were living in Omaha. I ended up learning about Keith's time in the NFL when people would come up to him while we were out. Keith never talked about it himself. I didn't even know he had played for the Cowboys until someone came up and asked, "What was it like to have missed getting a Super Bowl ring by one game?" Others commented on how his "injury became someone else's opportunity." (Emmitt Smith went on to become a hall-of-fame player.) Keith was so nonchalant in his responses. Several months into dating, I started asking Keith questions about his time playing. I asked if he had anything saved from those years. He said he had a couple videos, and his mom had a scrapbook. His humility grew more obvious, and so did my love for him.

CHAPTER 2
THE PRIVILEGE OF BREATHING

I OFTEN THINK ABOUT THE DAYS when my brother's roommate was playing basketball in Iowa and the racism he and the players from other countries endured from the opposing teams. It confused me then—as it does now—why people can be so resentful and fearful of others' successes. I didn't understand it at the time and never really will understand the thoughts or motivations of those who act on racial prejudice, but as I gain more experiences in life, it feels like I am getting better at understanding.

I don't think individuals see that they *themselves* are the root cause of what is driving their own prejudice. First, prejudice is taught, so it is often initially driven by emulating the behaviors, actions, and words of other people around them. In terms of the basketball games, these individuals had to plan in *advance*—they had to strategically coordinate and plan to bring bananas and an American flag to protest the Central American basketball player who was breaking records left and right in "their" small town.

If this record-breaking player were a white guy from small-town Iowa—despite being on a competing team—there would be nothing but love and respect. What is it about someone not like you, accomplishing things you may want, that stings so bad?

I think in many cases, these are individuals who believe they have predetermined limitations in their own lives that they will not get past. These limitations are reinforced by those in power who point the finger at minorities to deflect from the real source of inequality—their own accumulation of wealth, which is often powered and catapulted by insecurity. Those who have the means to acquire wealth often do so at the expense of others. But a poor white person will often see a rich white person and think, *I can have that if I try hard enough*, while that same individual will look at a person of color—rich or not—and think, *They're taking what's mine*.

A good example of this is the mixed response in 2018 to black high school student Michael Brown's full scholarship acceptances to twenty colleges, including four Ivy League schools. FOX News anchors Holly Morris and Sarah Fraser called Brown obnoxious for applying to so many schools and "taking a spot from someone else who worked really hard." The inferences of that statement are obvious. In their minds, Brown did not work hard even though he had a 4.68 GPA. He also, magically, would be taking multiple spots, even though he could only accept admission from and attend one school.

Quincy felt some of this in his own college experience. At UNL, many of the black students were there on athletic scholarships, and white students assumed he was a scholarship student too. However, while football was part of Quincy's past, he chose to step away in his college years. It was a decision he was privileged enough to make in comparison to Keith, whose drive to be the best and make it to the pros was fueled by a belief (and to some extent his reality) that earning a college education via a football scholarship was one of only a few roads that take him there; financial support from his parents was not an option.

Quincy's privilege is unique. He was raised with the privilege of living above the poverty line; expecting to get a car on his sixteenth birthday; always assuming there would be Christmas presents under the tree on Christmas morning; and knowing he would always, *always* have food to eat. He has a stepdad who played for the NFL, and even though it came with some unique complexities and downsides, the bottom line was that he had *two* dads involved in his life full time.

While Quincy was growing up, his dad and Keith spent hours in Keith's office playing cards and strategizing how to make Quincy a better player. Quincy's dad helped coach him starting in kindergarten and was his head coach from sixth grade through eighth grade. Then he followed Quincy to high school and joined the coaching staff there. Quincy always felt like he was only good because his dad was the coach, and other players sometimes said he had an unfair advantage. So when his dad left to coach at a rival school his sophomore year, Quincy felt relieved; he was going to be able to prove he could do it on his own. He began to realize with each play and carry, he was earning it, and his confidence grew. He played special teams just like Keith had—and at one of the most populated high schools in Nebraska where there was a high level of competition. The next year, his dad came back to coach him, and by then he had established he was doing it on his own.

Junior year, everything changed for Quincy. He and his teammates were caught smoking marijuana. Quincy's dad, Keith, and I had a plan for how to discipline Quincy, but his dad then decided his punishment should be through football. He was benched for three weeks, and then he still didn't get to play. Around the same time, Quincy's stepmom's nephew (with whom he was very close) died in a car accident. His passing was a paradigm shift for Quincy. It showed him how quickly things can change and taught him not to take people—or life itself—for granted. He was ready to take a step back and really focus on the things that had meaning to him, and it became clear that wasn't football.

When Quincy told me his heart wasn't in it, I felt like a terrible mom because I should have sensed this earlier. I should have encouraged him two or three years before to stop playing. When he finally quit, I kept asking if he was sure, because I didn't want him to have any regrets. But he really surprised me, and he confidently and repeatedly assured me that he was done. His senior year, he was at every game cheering on his team. He had the best time watching from the sidelines, free from the pressure of playing a role he was cast in but had never tried out for. Ever since I realized why he stopped playing, I've been really proud of him for saying no instead of continuing to do what others wanted him to. I've always believed that if you're going to do something, do it to your fullest potential.

It takes effort (let's call it *work*) and interest to embrace privilege. I know this because despite living side by side with my black and biracial family, I'm not always aware of my privilege. I am working hard, every day, to be better at this.

Jeanne Jones

I try to stay acutely aware of what my white privilege looks and feels like. It is so easy to have days, or possibly even a week, go by without intentionally trying to take a step back and think about the things in my life that can just simply *be*—not a second thought required. Consciously recognizing that not everyone navigates life with privilege.

Raising my daughters, it has been an honor for me to learn about the unique needs of caring for curly hair. I am not able to take my daughter down the street to just any "Hair Cuts For All" to spend a half hour in the salon, then have her walk out with her style of choice. Rather, my Sunday evenings usually consist of around three to four hours of washing, heavy conditioning, combing, parting and braiding. I am not good at it, and it is certainly not fun for my daughter. She cries almost every time, and recently she has been questioning why she is not "strong enough" (her words) to just deal with it. At her age, it certainly is confusing to her why her *twin sister* has a hair maintenance routine that consists of a wash, conditioner, and drying, then she can quickly and easily put it in a ponytail in the morning. Is it wrong to think about hair maintenance as privilege? My experience has been that the ease of access to hair care, the limited investment required, and a marketplace around every corner flooded with products that are designed for hair like mine is privilege.

✳ ✳ ✳

When you get in your car and drive down the street, do you worry about what your fate might be? I have never, ever worried about how I would be treated if I was pulled over by law enforcement, nor do I have expectations that I may be confronted, questioned, or even harmed for simply being present. If pulled over, I can rightfully expect to have the officer's treatment of me be consistent with the violation.

On the other hand, I worry about my son—as a young black man. Constantly. I worry about him because there have been too many cases such as that of Philando Castile, a young black man who was shot four times and killed by a Minnesota police officer while attempting to retrieve his driver's license as his girlfriend and her young daughter watched from the back seat. I worry about my son because of what happened to Breonna Taylor, an emergency medical technician, who was gunned down in her own home after police executed a no-knock search warrant in Louisville, Kentucky, and in the process sprayed over twenty bullets into the room, eight of which hit Breonna and killed her. The gunfire was said to be in response to her boyfriend, a licensed gun owner, firing a shot in response to what he believed was a break-in.

And more recently, in what is perhaps the most blatant and horrific account yet of murder at the hands of a law enforcement officer, is the case of George Floyd. We know through video evidence that George desperately pleaded for his life as he was restrained by Officer Derek Chauvin, who placed his left knee between George's head and neck. Having done my internship at the local police department, I am confident this officer knew that pressure on this area of the neck can be deadly, as there is a maneuver that is taught in self-defense training specifically targeting this area.

"I can't breathe," Mr. Floyd said, repeatedly. He pleaded for his mother, and he begged the officer, saying, "Please, please,

please," while Chauvin and other officers looked on and ignored his cries.

For eight minutes and forty-six seconds the knee stayed buried into George's neck. Six minutes in, George became non-responsive, yet Chauvin did not ease up. In videos of the incident, it captures him falling silent, bystanders urging the officers to check his pulse. They "couldn't find one," yet the officers did not take action to resuscitate.

At 20:27, Chauvin finally removed his knee from George's neck. He was taken to the Hennepin County Medical Center in an ambulance, and according to prosecutorial accounts, he was pronounced dead around an hour later.

It has not gone unnoticed that the "kneel" that ended George's life is symbolic of the reality of the injustice that is suffocating the entire black community as they navigate life with knees pressing into their necks. The response to the "unpatriotic" kneel by Colin Kaepernick—which cost him his career as he courageously fought to draw attention to the many injustices experienced every day in the black community—has been acknowledged by the NFL as a mistake, albeit in response to demands from the black players.

With each instance of overt injustice, I question how this can happen, and why there has not been more action to address the incidences of racial profiling and the differences between how law enforcement respond to blacks and minorities versus whites. This is not a personal theory or an opinion; it has been well researched, and the data suggests the gap is larger than many realize. According to MappingPoliceViolence.org, black men are more than three times as likely to be killed by a police officer than white men. Think about that. Typically, when one hears "three times as likely," it is viewed as pretty good odds. So when I put that in the context of my husband or sons' lives, those odds become increasingly unbearable to live with.

It is not just the treatment by law enforcement. The depth of social justice disparities are also manifested in how phrases used to describe situations involving blacks inherently support blatant assumptions that are not questioned and called out. An example of this is the use of these three words: unarmed black man. When Ahmaud Arbery is jogging and gets chased down and killed by two white men, why is there a need to qualify in the headline that the jogger was "an unarmed black man"? Calling out Ahmaud, and countless other black men before him, as being unarmed is an intentional move to address the implicit bias question that the media knows exists: "Was the man posing a threat?" This is a question that would not be proactively addressed for a white man.

In 1991 during my undergraduate studies, I took a class called Minorities in the Criminal Justice System. I was presented with facts that would have been convenient to place in short-term memory for test-taking purposes, then I could simply move on to the next class in pursuit of my degree. Instead, fact after fact that was presented left me astonished, ashamed, and enlightened to my ignorance. Unlike other classes of which I cannot recall much, this one has stayed top of mind throughout my life.

Thirty years later, I still remember how this class affected me—both physically and mentally. Although only twenty years old at the time, I was old enough to understand that the disparities being presented were deeply disturbing. I recall feeling a knot in my stomach after hearing some of the case studies.

This class helped me to have a better understanding of the blinders some of us are born with that continue to block our vision—until either chance, enlightenment, experience, or intentional effort is made on the part of the individual to seek to understand the experiences, differences and commonalities of those who are unlike them.

There is a reason why I'm kept up at night when my son is out. He has a different last name from mine, and his car is registered in my name. I have repeatedly reminded him of the protocol he must follow if he is ever pulled over (which, by the way, has never happened): (1) He is to put his hands on the steering wheel and do exactly what is asked of him; (2) When asked for his driver's license and registration, he is to immediately explain that this is his mother's car, that her last name is different than his and that he has one of her old IDs in his wallet that shows her name when it was the same as his. I make sure he has this ID, as he runs the risk of being accused of being in a stolen car and presenting a threat.

On his trips to and from the university he attended his freshman year, Quincy had to pass a barn with the president of the United States's name (at the time) plastered on the side of it. That name has been associated with support from the alt-right, which leads me to question if my son would be safe if he were to break down on the side of the road in the area. With the increases in hate-related crimes involving violence in recent years, having to ask this question is problematic, and it is a problem we should all be invested in.

The fact that the university Quincy attended defended and ignored violent threats against minorities and Jews as simply "political beliefs" was a clear indicator to me that tolerance for hate—at the leadership level—is being normalized. The lack of action taken at the highest level of our land after the death of Heather Heyer in Charlottesville, Virginia, on August 12, 2017, was one of the most prominent examples of this, and I believe it is correlated with the subsequent increases in hate-related violence. Even more troubling, so many cases go unreported (according to the Human Rights Campaign, over 54 percent of hate-related violence cases go unreported), and that the data is not telling the whole story. According to an NPR article dated November 12, 2019, "two of the most high-profile bias-motivated homicides in recent history were prosecuted as hate crimes, but never officially reported as such. The murders of Khalid Jabara in 2016 and Heather Heyer in 2017 were not included in FBI data, and their omissions prompted the introduction of the Jabara-Heyer NO HATE Act."

At times, I have heard hearing white friends or acquaintances respond in a dismissive manner to the reality of racial profiling or the uptick in hate-related violence. It astonishes me that there is an instinct to ignore the facts or minimize them at best. For example, when someone makes a comment like, "I have a friend who is black and they were telling me that they teach their kids to be respectful to prevent racial profiling or a confrontation," it affirms my point. White people do not have to give their white children detailed instruction on how to avoid an unprovoked confrontation with a police officer. Why? Because there is not likely to be one. However, it *is* likely that if a black person is arrested for the exact same crime as a white person, they will be convicted and have a more severe sentence than that their white counterpart.

Jeanne Jones

I run a red light, and the worst thought that goes through my mind is, *Oh boy, I may get a ticket.* But I also think, *I might get away with it,* because I have before. There were two instances when I drove from Kansas City to Omaha and was pulled over and given just a warning despite going 15 miles per hour over the speed limit. I recall being anxious about what this would mean for my insurance, but never for one moment was I scared or felt my life may be in danger.

How is it that two sets of human beings, living side by side in the same community, can expect to have a different experience than the other when it comes to how they are treated by our justice system because of the color of their skin? And in my case, two human beings, my son and I, sharing the same DNA, are experiencing different realities. In March 2019, the *Washington Post* reported on researchers who had compiled and analyzed data from more than 100 million traffic stops in the United States. They found police were more likely to pull over black drivers. The researchers were able to confirm racial bias by measuring daytime stops against nighttime stops, when darkness would make it more difficult to ascertain a driver's race. As with previous studies, they also found that black and Latino drivers are more likely to be searched for contraband—even though white drivers are consistently more likely to be found with contraband. They also found that legalization of marijuana in Colorado and Washington has caused fewer drivers to be searched during a stop, but that it did not alter the frequency in which black and Latino drivers are searched.[1]

Black men and boys are 2.5 times more likely than white men and boys to die during an encounter with the police, according to an August 16, 2019, article in the *LA Times.*[2] That number translates to 1 in every 1,000 young black men and boys; it tragically makes getting killed by police a leading cause of death for this demographic. If he were pulled over, Quincy's first thought is certainly not going to be, *Maybe if I am polite and smile they will let me off,* but rather, he will need to be on guard, aware, and well behaved so as not to signal to the police officer that he poses a threat. This is something that some with privilege have a hard time accepting as fact—that the instances of individuals being shot and killed by police officers are not just those involving confrontations or imminent threat but also those triggered by implicit bias.

There is a moment burned in my memory—another alarming, sobering moment that has enabled me to see more clearly the systemic unconscious bias that exists in our country.

I was making cookies for the girls, and the night was off to a great start. I was in a job where I was traveling every week, so being home and doing something this simple, together, was something to cherish. I caught the headline first, then I asked my husband to turn up the TV so I could hear. I listened as the news reporter described an event that happened the day before at a presidential rally. A black man who had been protesting at the rally was being escorted out of the auditorium by a police officer when a white man approached him and punched him in the face. In other words—the white man physically assaulted him, which is a crime and should have resulted in an immediate arrest. Unlike peacefully protesting, which is not a crime. Instead of immediately arresting the white assaulter who had just committed this crime in front law enforcement, the police officer instead continued to forcibly remove the black man from the auditorium for *peacefully protesting.* There was absolutely no visible instinct to arrest the white man who assaulted the black man in front of him. Instead, the officer's instincts told him to get the black man out, because he was seen as a "threat." It was important to me to ensure Quincy watched this video, and we had a conversation about what he needed to take away from it should he ever find himself in a similar position. Holding back tears and maintaining a serious tone to ensure I had his attention, I asked him to explain to me what it meant to him. He went on to share surprising insights on how he is perceived and why it didn't take that video for him to know that when punched by a white guy in front of law enforcement not to expect help. At this moment I was confronted with the fact that my son had been living out this scenario already as simply a reality of his existence, while I had been living in a false reality predicated on my own experiences being privileged and protected.

It would seem that one of the most meaningful ways to help overcome blindness to privilege would be to begin to teach children at an early age that their minds will naturally have unconscious biases, and that there are techniques they can use to help grow a greater awareness of its implications. Imagine the progress that could be made if parents made an effort—during the same time they are teaching their children about the dangers of not looking before crossing a street, not touching a hot stove, or not petting a strange dog—to educate their children using analogies they can understand about implicit bias. Not being born a target of implicit bias is privilege.

The Perception Institute breaks down the term *implicit bias* in the following way: "Thoughts and feelings are 'implicit' if we are unaware of them or mistaken about their nature. We have a bias when, rather than being neutral, we have a preference for (or aversion to) a person or group of people. Thus, we use the term 'implicit bias' to describe when we have attitudes towards people or associate stereotypes with them without our conscious knowledge."[3]

Studies have shown individuals report a higher perception of risk and threat when a black person is confronted versus a white person. In what Stanford sociology professor Jennifer L. Eberhardt refers to as *attentional bias*, "we've shown that black faces are much more likely to capture the attentional systems of those who have been induced to think about crime than those who have not. It is as if the existing stereotypic association between blacks and crime renders these faces more perceptually relevant and therefore worthy of being seen."[4] Said another way, when an officer pulls Quincy over, he is likely to view him skeptically even before either of them open their mouths.

Quincy drove to Kansas City recently to see his dad and attend a Kansas City Chiefs game. It is about a three-hour drive from our home, and he left at 9:00 p.m. I had constant anxiety until I got his text that he had made it safe. If he had gotten a flat tire, he would have been in an almost entirely rural, white area that (according to the Southern Poverty Law Center monitoring) has pockets of hate groups. What if he were pulled over to the side of the road, and a truck with an American flag and gun rack on top had stopped to help him? These could be kind people in a rural town who just want to help. However, with the increasing instances of hate crimes and brazen displays of outward hostility toward minorities, my mind goes to the worst of places. Just when I tell myself that I am bordering on paranoia and my fears are not real, there is another news story about the increase in hate crimes. In fact, on November 12, 2019, the *New York Times* published a story regarding an FBI annual report, which stated, "personal attacks motivated by bias or prejudice reached a sixteen-year high in 2018," and "while crimes against property were down, physical assaults against people were up, accounting for 61 percent of the 7,120 incidents classified as hate crimes by law enforcement officials nationwide."[5]

This was published *after* compiled FBI data indicated a 17 percent increase in reported hate crime incidents between 2016 and 2017. *Whew!* What also needs to be considered is that cities and states are not required to report hate crimes to the FBI, and "many cities and some entire states failed to collect or report the data during [2016 to 2017]." The November 12, 2019 *New York Times* report went on to conclude, "the trends show more violence [and] more interpersonal violence."[6] I ask myself, *If all instances had been reported, what would this number look like?* With 61 percent of these incidents being violent in nature, how do I prepare my children?

Keith and I had an experience at a local car dealership recently in which we were blatantly ignored by the sales staff and watched as they quickly greeted every other (white) customer who had come on the lot. My guess is they assumed that we could not afford one of their cars and that attending to us would be a waste of time. I have also observed how much more closely our actions are monitored when I'm shopping with our kids, especially since Quincy has gotten older. This is just another experience of which many people question the reality. Or they may question the frequency. They may say, "Yes it happens, but it is the exception and not the rule." It is real, and it is not an exception. It takes effort, interest, and empathy to observe from a different lens. When those who are not subjected to daily discrimination do this, it can be powerful. Especially when there is advocacy; if you see it, say something. Empathy without action is not helpful.

Keith frequently takes walks in our almost entirely white neighborhood that we have lived in for over ten years. About a year ago, he was walking his normal route when he ran into some of the neighborhood boys playing in the street. They saw him and one yelled, "Robber! Run!" It is not uncommon for black people to have to endure being viewed as criminals when they are in predominantly white areas, minding their own business. There have been more news stories in the past two years than I can count featuring a video of a white person calling the police because they see a black person in their neighborhood, or at their pool, or most notably but not uncommonly, in their Starbucks. The most disturbing yet is the case of Ahmaud Arbery, which hit very close to home for Keith. On one of his recent walks, which are essential for Keith to take to prolong his degenerative condition, he was followed by a truck with a gun rack that slowly crept behind him and would not pass him. We were together when we first watched the video of Ahmaud being shot and killed by the men in the trucks that were chasing him down like a wild animal. We didn't speak; we watched in silence, but we knew we were both thinking the same thing: *It could have been him*. It shook us to the core. I think about how many people watch this video and can have empathy in the moment, then walk away from it, knowing the personal impact to them does not stretch beyond the news segment. Empathy is not enough, there must be advocacy.

Questions like, "What were they doing there?" and "Is he or she a criminal?" are rooted in implicit bias. It is worth repeating: Don't our children deserve to learn about implicit bias at a young age, so they can avoid unintentional—yet hurtful—responses such as this? Don't we as a society have an obligation, when we know there are huge cracks in our foundation, to fix them to prevent fellow human beings from falling into these cracks?

Eberhardt stresses that bias, while detrimental when left unchecked, stems from positive evolutionary processes: "Categorization…is not some abhorrent feature of the human brain, a process that some people engage in and others do not. Rather, it is a universal function of the brain that allows us to organize and manage the overload of stimuli that constantly bombard us."[7] We categorize things every day—types of clothing, types of animals, types of foods. The danger comes when our categorizations become stereotypes and affect how we perceive and treat others. For instance, black men and women on government assistance may be perceived to be lazy and working the system, while white men and women on that same assistance may be perceived as outliers; one thinks, *Something devastating must have happened*, as opposed to, *They are taking advantage of the system*. I've observed both firsthand.

Jamie Foxx once shared in an interview that his father was arrested and sentenced to seven years in prison for getting caught with twenty-five dollars' worth of an illegal substance on his person. *Seven years*. There is no middle-class white person who could ever imagine spending seven years in prison for a minor, *malum in se* crime. If there are a few cases like this, they are by far an exception, not the rule. During high school, if any of my classmates were caught with marijuana, the worst of their fears was being benched from a sport, kicked out of a club, or getting slapped on the wrist. There would be outrage by parents and headlines in the news if they were handed a seven-year prison sentence. Yet, for minorities in the criminal justice system, one would always have to be prepared to expect the worst.

There is case after case of disparate sentences being handed down to minorities. It is called injustice, and to this day, thirty years after I was first introduced to my Minorities in the Criminal Justice System course, the data continues to show the same gaps. The laws of our criminal justice system are designed to penalize minorities. The American Civil Liberties Union stated in a 2013 report that "marijuana use is roughly equal among blacks and whites, yet blacks are 3.73 times as likely to be arrested for marijuana possession."[8] I pointed out "three times as likely" as great odds; 3.73 times as likely is statistically significant and cannot be ignored.

Currently, as marijuana has become legal in eleven states as of 2020, white entrepreneurs are becoming billionaires while black Americans remain incarcerated, many with life sentences. According to *USA Today*, "The top tier of the legal pot industry run almost exclusively by white men, and retailers, dispensaries and pharmacies nationwide are expected to take in nearly $45 billion in revenue by 2024 from all cannabinoid sales."[9] By contrast, most black sellers make only enough to get by and provide the basic necessities for their families. In 2018, in states that still banned marijuana use at the time, only 11 percent of offenders that were given federal sentences were white, even though whites make up over 60 percent of the population in the United States.[10] I reflect on my son's experience having been caught by us, his parents, with marijuana and wonder what the consequences may have been for him if he were caught by law enforcement. We benched him from football, and he paid the price at home, but what sentence may have been handed down if it were under different circumstances? As a black male, he's not allowed to experiment without extreme consequences that could derail his entire life.

Implicit bias is also extremely prevalent in how news is delivered. With the rise in mass shootings by white men, the headlines will often seek to understand the shooter and lead with an assumption that this man must have had a condition or circumstance that drove him to commit the horrific crime. By contrast, black males who commit crimes are often called "thugs," (this word being inexcusably and disturbingly used by POTUS on Twitter), and they are characterized as resisting, while Middle Eastern–presenting males are characterized as potential terrorists. An article in *Yes!* magazine shows this disparity, along with other examples of white privilege, using pictures from news outlets as examples.

I do not recall ever seeing a news headline highlighting the positive attributes of a black male suspect. Yet, not infrequently, white suspects are depicted in a positive light and are usually framed in the media as honorable citizens. A real example highlighted in the *Yes!* article has a picture of a white male murder suspect. He is in a professional photo wearing a suit and tie; his photo is accompanied by a headline labeling him as a "brilliant science student." This is in contrast to Michael Brown's picture with him in a red basketball jersey, flashing a sign; his photo is accompanied by a headline reading "struggled with officer," as to suggest he deserved to be murdered.[11]

To further illustrate the disparities in the presentation of cases involving white and black suspects, one can compare two sets of pictures featured in a Cedar Rapids, Iowa, KCRG 9 ABC news segment. The photos featuring the white suspects are most likely their student athlete photos, taken by professional photographers with all men wearing suits and ties. The photos featuring the black suspects are their mugshots. These photos and articles are reporting on the same crime, covered by the same reporter on the same day! Take a minute to think about this. Why would mugshots be used in one situation and not the other? One set of men were depicted as violent criminals, and the other as college students.

✳✳✳

ON HYPOCRISY

I OFTEN WONDER what life would have been like for me without the experiences I had with other cultures and races. Would I be able to support, or simply overlook, a president who is divisive and lacks moral character? I like to believe that would never be the case, because I was raised by the kindest, most angelic woman I've ever known. Plain and simple, she taught me right from wrong, and to not turn a blind eye to racism and bullying. I have a father who repeatedly preached to us about all the things *not* to be: Don't be a liar. Don't cheat (in *any* form, but especially on a spouse). Don't bully and call people names. Don't discriminate. Don't judge people by their religion or appearance. My father was impassioned when making comments like, "I will not allow a liar in my house," or calling out narcissist and cheating behavior as intolerable and disgusting. It is so incomprehensible that all the things I was raised *not* to be, that I was taught were fundamentally wrong, are behaviors that the leaders in our country seem to be overlooking, dismissing, and in too many cases even possessing today. And many of my father's generation, like him, are turning a blind eye to the immoral behavior, narcissism, and lack of values we see today at the highest office in our land. I am repeatedly asking myself, *What is driving this? How can this be?* And, most importantly, *How can I teach my children right from wrong when there is an alternate universe blurring these lines and conveniently making exceptions to truth?*

As positive as it was to experience in my lifetime a two-term black U.S. president—President Barack Obama—it was eye opening for me to simultaneously experience "birtherism" and the cold reality of the deep-seated racism that initiated, facilitated, and continues to foster it. It must come down to the underlying fear of losing privilege; there is really no other explanation for it.

My privilege is also apparent when considering employment. When applying for a job, even as a woman, I am able to make the assumption that my resume will not be set aside because of my name sounding "ethnic." My niece, Ebony Jones, for example, may not be afforded this same level of confidence that her resume will be looked at objectively. A 2015 Pew Research Center study showed that "college-educated black and Hispanic men earn roughly 80 percent the hourly wages of white college-educated men ($25 and $26 vs. $32, respectively)."[12] What a significant gap to overcome! Khan Academy introduces another alarming statistic: I could have a prison record and still be two to three times more likely to be offered a job than would a black man with no record at all.[13] This is the sad reality I am preparing my sons and daughters to expect, but not accept. To *not have to* prepare your children to expect less pay for the same work is a *privilege*. This is important data that deserves to be understood, accepted, and talked about in an effort to move the needle.

The 2019 college admissions bribery scandal really underscored the immense disparity in privilege in our country; it showed how those with connections can give their children a leg up even before those children enter the workforce. What the parents involved in the scandal did was against the law—plain and simple—and they deserve prosecution. Some of these individuals responded in an accountable way that should be applauded and emulated. For example, originally Felicity Huffman had psychologically justified to herself that paying $15,000 for a false SAT score for her daughter was not wrong—because she was motivated by helping her child achieve success. After being confronted with the illegality of her actions—and serving time for the offense—she became utterly and completely contrite about her actions. She accepted her punishment and acknowledged she was not viewing her actions from a lens of privilege but rather from a lens of love for her daughter. When there is ownership and accountability, we should embrace it and share the positivity that comes with learning, not simply focus on the negative.

I think for many, and maybe even most (because I do believe there are more good, honorable people than not), this highlights the realities of privilege. By contrast, one would question if Lori Loughlin has the ability to see her privilege for what it is. Accused of a similar crime to Felicity Huffman, she purportedly told sources close to her that she was just doing what any mother would do. If this is true, she fails to recognize the privilege of being able to spend an exorbitant amount of money to ensure her children attend the school of her choice (via a criminal act) versus earning a fair admission. I would argue mothers who understand privilege would push their children to be their best, focusing on teaching them that they will be given what they earn. If I sound repetitive, it is intentional. How will our children know this if we do not teach them? Education is imperative for change.

For those who are ready to tackle their own unconscious bias, Vanderbilt University's website lists some strategies to mitigate it (see next page).

- Learn as Much as Possible About Unconscious Bias… and Ways to Combat It

- Tell Your Story…and Listen to the Stories of Others

- Avoid Stereotypes and Over-Generalizations

- Separate Feelings from Facts

- Have a Diverse Group of People around the Decision-Making Table

- Engage in Self-Reflection to Uncover Personal Biases

- Develop Safe and Brave Spaces to Discuss Unconscious Bias

- Be an Active Ally

- Don't Expect a Quick Fix

- Practice Empathy[14]

CHAPTER 3
THE WORTH OF A LIFE

KEITH AND I HAD BEEN DATING for just a couple of months when I invited him over for a late dinner. He did not get out of work most nights until well past 11:00 p.m., so it had become the norm for me to stay up and have dinner ready for both of us to enjoy for the hour or so before I had to call it a night. I worked the more traditional, yet still demanding, hours of 7:30 a.m. to about 6:00 p.m., so we cherished the time together when we had it.

I had made Keith steak on the George Foreman grill, a baked potato, and asparagus on the side. We were at that critical time in an emerging relationship when we needed to start asking the tough questions and gauging our long-term compatibility. On this night, I opened up to Keith about my constant struggle with following a religion out of obligation—one that seemed to have already condemned me to hell based on my divorce and not getting married in the church, amongst other "sins" I had committed. I felt sharing this with him was a risk; many people are very set in their faiths, and a lack of conviction could be a game changer. I had no idea the conversation would ultimately become the glue that bonds us together.

Many conversations would follow throughout the years in which we attempted to unravel the complex dimensions of the varied religious faiths and how religion has been historically tied to race and oppression. As I embark on this topic I want to be clear: I have enormous respect for religions throughout the world and personally practice and appreciate the power of faith. We are raising our children to be spiritual and supportive of the different faiths of family, friends, and loved ones. Having said this, it has become increasingly clear to me that I cannot advocate for human rights and social justice and not call out the complacency we as a country have witnessed amongst religious communities not rising up to denounce systemic racism despite the long-standing historical imperative to do so.

Growing up, I learned and practiced a religion that had so many rules, and I did not always see the correlation between the rule and the ties to being a good human being. I found myself questioning, *How does this make me a good person?* or *How does this help people?* These are questions that I have grown to repeatedly ask myself during my journey to seek to understand how religious practices tie to everyday values and beliefs.

Like with many religions, I was taught to believe that mine was the "correct" one, and other religions were somehow not valued as truth. This was an easy belief for me to uphold—or anyone in my community—because, according to the Pew Research Center, Christians make up 75 percent of Nebraskans' belief systems, with Catholics pretty much equally sharing that percentage with Evangelical Protestants and Mainline Protestants.[15] When I accompanied my mother to the grocery store and saw the concern in the grocer's eyes about us having enough to eat—and his insistence that she take what she need and pay for it later—I now look back and wonder if his response would have been different had we been brown-skinned with hijabs. Would he have felt the same connection to a family of another religion?

Similarly, my father's religion-based vow of poverty didn't ostracize us from our community. In fact, Boys Town is a long-standing establishment in our town that was founded by a Catholic priest, and it was able to pass down household items to us with no reservation, thanks to generous donors. While other religious institutions charitably support their members as well, they often have less to pass down to begin with, because they start with less. In this sense, though poor, I was a recipient of religious privilege, enveloped within the membership of an "acceptable" faith.

My fond memories of my mother are strongly connected to the religious beliefs in which she held, and the example of faith she set. While I no longer practice religion the way I was raised, it doesn't bother me to see religious symbols. Like most of America, religious or not, I still celebrate Christmas. In this way I am still a recipient of Christian privilege even while no longer practicing. I do not live in a country that colonized my people and forced us to reject our faith on the grounds of their own. My children don't have to draw caricatures of their culture on Thanksgiving or have people look at them sideways if they celebrate Ramadan. Even if I didn't teach my children the basics of religion to give them an understanding of others, they would still grow up with knowledge of Christianity simply because of their surroundings. And, as *Relevant* magazine points out, people like me (and especially my father), still have more Christian privilege than, say, people like Keith ever did. In their article "Does Christian Privilege Really Exist? (in America, It Depends on Your Skin Color)," they state:

> Where is this alleged Christian privilege for people of color in America? Does it prevent the current administration from ending DACA? Has it stopped the anti-Mexican rhetoric from the White House? Has it made a difference or slowed the gunning down of young, unarmed black men who brandish mobile phones that officers mistook as firearms, resulting in six shots to the back? Community churches in Oakland; Sacramento; Brooklyn; Houston; Sanford, Florida; and Waller County, Texas, grieve the loss of their friends, family, children and loved ones. I wonder how privileged they feel?[16]

✳ ✳ ✳

The basis of many faiths that are predominate in America center around "doing the right thing," avoiding "sinning," and at the core, deeply loving and caring for one another, placing the highest value on human life. With these simplistic foundational guideposts, it becomes hard to understand how those that are losing their lives to social injustice can be completely disregarded, while there is such strong motivation, advocacy, and strategy around protecting the lives of the unborn. The rationale behind this is something that I have consistently struggled with. Why is an unborn life more important than my husband's life? Those of my sons? Those of the workers in the fields and in the factories across our country that are such an important part of our economy?

In the months leading up the 2016 presidential election, I had many conversations with coworkers, friends, and family about my concerns with the consistently racist behaviors and dog whistles that were emerging from one of the candidates. My pleas to think about the ramifications of a person like this leading our country, and how deeply impacted my family would be, were met with an opposing view that not overturning abortion would be dramatically worse, and that all other moral considerations could be set aside to promote this interest. Years later, here we are. In a place that is continuing to progress in the direction of my worst-case scenarios; blatant injustice is being ignored at the highest office in our land, and the religious organizations are standing by silently.

Because this is not new, we have to take a look back and try to better understand how religions throughout our country's history have allowed injustices to prevail for hundreds of years. The history of race and religion in America is deeply complex, as they are two independent constructs that intersect, with race being socially engineered as a means to classify people, promote supremacy, and foster financial gain.

Racial engineering, to this day, has led to the disparities that we have not yet been able to overcome as a country. A report published in January 2019 by the Institute for Policy Studies found the median black family owns $3,600, which represents 2 percent of the median white family's wealth. Similarly, the median Latino family owns $6,600, which is 4 percent of the median white family.[17] According to a 2013 report by the Sentencing Project, black males are six times more likely to be incarcerated than white males.[18] At that rate, 1 in 3 black males will go to prison, compared with 1 in 17 white males. Although the president has frequently touted record low unemployment rates for black people, they still have the highest rates of unemployment, and black women die in maternity-related deaths at three times that of white women. The data highlights broad injustices, and the lack of solutions that have been generated to make positive movement toward equality speaks to the complexity.

I don't have the answers. I wish I did. I am consistently struggling with how to make a difference when confronting a topic that is deeply personal to some, but in my opinion is deeply flawed. On any given day, one of the most frequent thoughts I have is: *Why is it so hard to view the world from a different lens, consciously and briefly, just once a day?* Think about the power in that. If someone who currently singularly focuses on the right to life for the unborn—willingly excusing and ignoring immoral behaviors by our leaders in an effort to accomplish this ultimate goal of protecting human life—would make an effort once a day to listen to the stories of the mothers who have lost their sons, families separated from their loved ones, anyone who can share a story on an unjust life lost, and put this in the same perspective as unborn life lost, wouldn't and shouldn't this lead to the same compassion and advocacy?

Unfortunately, I don't believe so. Why? Because of that intersection that exists between race and religion. *Without this intersection,* a life is a life, there would be no differentiation whatsoever. We are forced to admit as a country, when race is introduced as a factor in the right to life, the implicit bias deep in our psyche allows the compartmentalization of immigrants and black and brown people, enabling the differentiation from unborn babies.

Although with much less serious consequences, I experience this same compartmentalization and differentiation coming from those who are "fans" of my husband. Recently my daughter had pulled up a YouTube video of Keith doing a football interview with another former Husker, Tommie Frazier, and a local radio personality. She was reading out loud the comments from the fans and one stood out to me:

> I am so glad to see Keith Jones again! I really enjoyed watching him play back in the late 1980s. I will never forget the touchdown that he scored against OU in 1987, which gave me such hope that the Huskers would finally beat OU that year (which unfortunately did not happen that year) and Keith Jones' huge day (248 yards, I think?) against CU the following weekend was epic. Keith "End Zone" Jones is a true Husker legend.

The fan views Keith from the lens of a football player, a "true Husker legend." I wonder if this fan ever thinks about how Keith must be constantly on guard while taking a walk in his own neighborhood. Or how Keith gets stared down by strangers at a stoplight, shaking their heads at him in disgust just for the color of his skin. (*Why is that black man driving a car that is nicer than mine?*) Compartmentalization allows fans to conveniently dismiss the everyday realities Keith must confront being a black man in America. Imagine if this were not the case and fans across the country—as they were cheering on the black athletes that make up the foundation of the NCAA and most professional sports leagues—associated accomplishments like each touchdown, or basket, or home run with the historical context that it deserves; these are people who continue to be oppressed and marginalized yet courageously move forward each day in a world that has not yet gotten beyond oppression of their people.

CHAPTER 4
BLENDING FAMILIES, BLENDING WORLDS

WHEN I TOLD MY DAD I WAS MARRYING KEITH, he said that he was resentful when his mom got remarried after his dad had died. Even though my dad was an adult when his mom remarried, he carried that bitterness with him. He told me Quincy would become a juvenile delinquent because I was putting another man before Q. He said if I really cared about my son, I wouldn't remarry. Even though I knew my mom had brought Keith into my life, my dad's words rang in the back of my mind for years. I was always working overtime to help Quincy see the balance in our blended family, and to ensure he viewed it as a gift to have a stepfather who was so involved in his life and who cared deeply about him. When he graduated from high school with a 3.91 GPA, earning 18 college-level credits through the local university, while being a student athlete, working part time, and not spending a single minute of all those years in detention, I felt like I could breathe a sigh of relief that my decision didn't ruin his life. I always carried this constant fear of Quincy believing I was putting someone else in front of him. That was a difficult dynamic for Keith and me to work through.

My dad's job clouded his vision about non-traditional families. Working at Boys Town, he saw young men acting out daily, and many of them came from broken homes. But our home wasn't broken. I had chosen Keith very carefully, with my mom's blessing. He was a gift from her.

In my heart, I knew I was giving Quincy a good role model and an amazing example of the man he could become. Quincy's dad remains in his life, which we have encouraged. Keith and I both wanted them to have a relationship that was strong and healthy. It was also really important to me that I raise Quincy in a positive environment, one with high expectations for reaching his full potential. I always told him how special he was and how there was a uniqueness about him. He was born with a birthmark on his leg in the shape of a four-leaf clover, which I used as evidence of this uniqueness and of how lucky I was to be his mom.

Race wasn't much of an issue when he was young. Racism is taught, and until children learn how to differentiate and categorize race, it is simply not a thing. Q had black friends, white friends, and even biracial friends. In middle school, the dynamics changed a bit. He was suddenly more aware of how he was different from his classmates. Inner-city kids were bussed from North Omaha—where Keith had grown up—and from other underserved areas. Many of the bussed students were black and Hispanic, and most of the other students were white and middle class. Quincy was biracial and middle class, so he didn't fit in completely with either dynamic.

To complicate things further, Quincy was better off financially than many of his black and biracial classmates. The income
disparity in Omaha is significant. According to City-Data.com,
the median African American household income in Omaha in
2017—the year Quincy graduated—was $32,729, compared
to $79,045 for the white residents, or over double.[19]

I was raised below the poverty line, which affected how Q
was being raised. He had this unique dynamic of being between
two races and two socioeconomic realities, which he encoun-
tered regularly when spending time with his grandfather, aunts,
uncles, and cousins. I'm really cheap when it comes to spending
money on myself: I take bargain shopping to the extreme, use
electronic coupons and discounts on apps, and rarely spend
more than fifteen dollars for a pair of shoes on clearance. But for
Quincy, I didn't mind spending unnecessarily. I wanted him to
have what I didn't. That said, I also didn't want him to take his
good fortune for granted and desperately wanted him to appreciate what it is like for those that go without. I started babysitting
at twelve years old, working at fourteen years old, and I have
been working full-time hours consistently since sixteen years old;
I was adamant about instilling that same work ethic in Quincy.
Leading up to his fifteenth birthday, we constantly reminded
Q that he needed to find a job for the summer, or he would
not have a summer. When school let out without him having
secured a job, Keith and I held true to our commitment, and
he spent the first three weeks of his summer vacation grounded.
He found a job as a referee to third graders at a recreational
basketball center and got firsthand experience as to how "pas-
sionate" parents can be about their children. He couldn't believe
how many parents cursed him out over what they perceived as

bad calls. This was an opportunity to help him understand how differently people can view the world when they come from an intentionally limited or entitled perspective. Sometimes what is black and white—and what is obvious to everyone around—can be completely overlooked or challenged due to a personal desire to have one's own experience be the *only* experience. What an important life lesson.

Although we had high expectations for Quincy working, Keith naturally questioned my logic about spoiling him with material things, and my actions almost ended up costing me our marriage. Quincy went through a stage where he was obsessed with Air Jordans and would spend hours researching the different versions and following new releases. When he was a freshman in high school, he asked me to buy him a certain pair that was coming out. He knew they were going to sell out right away at the stores in the major cities, and we would only be able to get them on eBay—even though they were even more pricey there. He begged and begged, and against my better judgement, I finally gave in.

This was a mistake—a huge mistake. Because once I gave in this first time, it became harder to say no, and it seemed like a new version was being released every month. At some point along the way, Q must have intuitively connected that if he mentioned me favoring Keith over him when he asked for things, the conversation would ultimately end with a yes regarding whatever he wanted. He was very in tune with the constant guilt I was shouldering over his accusations that I was picking Keith over him and "ruining his life" by choosing "my happiness" over his. After the first yes, Keith questioned why he needed these expensive shoes (we both grew up wearing worn out shoes with holes), and it became difficult to justify another pair. Q and I ended up agreeing to ship a different pair of shoes to my sister's house, to keep them hidden from Keith and avoid a confrontation. It felt like the right solution at the time. However, not surprisingly, Keith eventually found out. He had confiscated Quincy's phone during a punishment and had read texts between Q and me about the shoes.

To say there was a blow-up over those damn shoes was an understatement. Keith was upset because we were conspiring behind his back about something we knew he would never agree with. I had broken his trust. Trust that—for two people who had been through multiple relationships without it—meant absolutely everything to us. I could have argued that I never actually lied, and that I just didn't tell him because I didn't think it would be important for him to know. But *that* would have been a lie. So instead, I tried to help him understand my thought process, and I shared for the first time that nagging voice in my head telling me, *You are picking a man over your son and his life will be ruined for it.* In time, Keith began to not only better understand how this had been influencing my decision-making, but he also began to help me understand that I cannot let the experiences and judgements of others mold me. If I believed in him—and I had no doubts that he was the best role model for my son—how could I allow someone else's experiences to become a self-fulfilling prophecy? Jordan-gate will go down as one of the biggest tests to our marriage, and we survived it with some common truths that we now hold close: I am highly protective of Quincy. (He is my first born, and for the longest time it was just him and me against the world!) I will always have a voice in my head checking me (now in a healthy way) to ensure

I am prioritizing him, but now it will not question my decision to marry the man I knew would be the best father ever. Lastly, I would continue to want to give Q and all our children the things my mom longed to give me but couldn't, and that is okay.

✳ ✳ ✳

My stepson Kaydon has been a joy. I couldn't have asked for a better stepson. Although we do not get to see him nearly as often as we would like, he is kind and reserved and our love for him runs deep. Kaydon is in a tough spot; he has in Quincy an older stepbrother who is with us full time, so when he comes to stay, it always takes a minute to settle in. The girls worship him and love to tease him and hang out with him. They call him Shrek and he takes it all in stride. Kaydon never asks for anything—I always have to initiate questions about what he may want or need. Kaydon's experience is almost the opposite of Quincy's. He didn't feel the pressure to play football at a young age, he didn't play for the first time until high school. Instead, his interests were in track and basketball. Kindergarten through sixth grade, he attended a predominately white Catholic elementary school, and he is now attending an all-boys Catholic high school that is also predominately white. As helpful as we believe this will be in the long term to prepare him to enter the workforce as a minority, whether in Omaha or elsewhere, it comes with the trade-off of being surrounded daily by different religious practices than your own (Kaydon is Baptist) and students who do not look like you.

Unlike their brothers' experiences, Ezley and Xonya will undoubtedly benefit and experience privilege being raised in the same household with both their biological parents. We have had a great experience having them attend the same diverse elementary school Quincy did. As twins, they are as different as you can possibly imagine, and not just physically. Ezley was born an artist, and it shines through in so many ways. From a young age, she began to draw complex, themed pictures, and within a week after getting her first sketchbook, she already had a clothing line established. She loves facials, hand balm, lip gloss, and shopping. Like her brother, she can quickly and easily break me down, and I end up spending frivolously on things that are wants and not needs. Xonya is introverted and into sports. She doesn't care if she matches and has grown to love athleisure clothes and anything rainbow. Like Kaydon, she rarely expresses wanting things. Most recently, she has begun throwing the football around with Keith and wants to start playing so she can break down stereotypes and barriers for women.

Keith has been hard on Quincy and Kaydon as young men, and over the years I have come to better understand why—his own dad wasn't around growing up. He felt like he needed to do all the things a dad should do that he hadn't experienced himself—the things he knew were important. Because we do not get to see Kaydon often during the school year, it is a struggle to apply the rules and discipline over the course of short stays. Keith has been very intentional about instilling his work ethic in Kaydon and challenging him to achieve his full potential.

Our most trying time with Quincy happened right after his high school graduation. We had pretty strict house rules, just like I did when I was his age. After graduation, he declared to Keith and me that he was going to start coming and going as he pleased and not adhere to our rules anymore. He and Keith got in a heated argument, and Quincy, to my horror, told Keith for the first time, "You're not my dad." This was especially hurtful to Keith, because he had been in Quincy's life fully since Q was six years old. When we went through all those trying times as a family, and I saw Quincy upset, I always wanted to fast-forward so he could see things in hindsight. I think he does understand it now. From my perspective, I see that Quincy always sets the tone and pace with his peers. He never seemed to find the opinions of others important. As Keith has said since he first met him, "Quincy marches to the beat of his own drum."

In high school, Quincy had an internal battle about whether to hang with the black kids from North Omaha or assimilate with the white kids. He didn't think either the white or black kids were better. He just saw the disparity and felt like he was forced to make a choice between one of two groups.

Growing up biracial, he experienced the stereotypes on both sides. His good friend Davon is black, and he has many friends from Omaha's black community. Davon played basketball and football for inner-city leagues, and many of his teammates were black and underserved. Devon would tell Quincy his friends saw him as white. They'd call him "the light-skinned one," or "the whitewash." But the white students saw him as black. While it's difficult in a way I'll never know firsthand, he's also told me that being biracial makes a person understand both sides and connect to both, even if the rest of the world sees them as the opposite of whatever they are themselves.

I got pregnant with Ezley and Xonya when Quincy was in sixth grade. Quincy had asked for siblings when he was younger, but he wasn't quite as excited by the time it became a reality. In addition to the not-so-great news about adding two baby girls to the family, Quincy's two best friends had both recently moved out of state within a short time of each other. Then just weeks after the twins were born, our dog died suddenly in a Fourth of July accident. It was a tough time.

I started showing signs of preterm labor at thirty-two weeks. On a Tuesday morning, I was admitted to the hospital to slow the labor down. At this point, the girls were fine—moving and kicking and plugging along. That morning, they weighed me and had me do a urine sample. I saw what I thought was blood in the cup. I left it in the bathroom like I was told, but the day went on and no one came to pick it up. Finally it got discarded, but without anyone testing it. That probably would have been the first sign of what would turn out to be preeclampsia. Left untreated, preeclampsia moves to eclampsia and then to HELLP syndrome. Most women die at this last stage.

Over the next few days, my body started swelling and my legs were like tree trunks. I had seen this before: my mom's legs looked just like this right before she needed dialysis, because her body was retaining water. Her kidney failure was a complication of diabetes, which runs strong on both sides of my family. My grandfather lost both his legs to diabetes and died from diabetes-related complications. My uncle recently passed away after years of dealing with diabetic complications.

Despite my family history, no one listened when I said I didn't look normal. No one took my weight. Part of the confusion might have been that high blood pressure is a common symptom and trigger of eclampsia, and my blood pressure continued to be steady and always stayed lower than 130. But I think it was also the way I was being perceived—as "naturally" heavy and advanced maternal age.

My OB-GYN was on vacation, so I was being treated by doctors who didn't know me. They wanted to send me home with a bolus pump on Friday night. My preterm labor had slowed down, and they said I could administer the medicine myself with the pump. Keith and I had all our stuff ready to go home, but my sister was furious. She went up to the nurses' station and tried to fight on my behalf.

"She shouldn't look like this. You can't send her home," she argued. They conceded, and I remained in the hospital.

The next morning was June 12— my mother's birthday. My swelling was getting increasingly worse, and I was having difficulty breathing when a nurse named Angel came in. Of course her name was Angel, and I met her on my mom's birthday.

"How much weight have you gained since you've been here?" she asked.

"No one weighed me," I said, "so I'm not sure."

"When did they check you in?"

"Tuesday morning."

I saw her jaw drop. I showed her my legs and told her about my mom dying from kidney failure. Angel weighed me, and I had gained over 10 pounds in water weight in just five days. On a 5'3"-inch frame that went into the pregnancy weighing 125 pounds, this was significant.

Right away they got a catheter going to get some of the fluid out, and they started running tests. They brought in a machine to check my heart and lungs. I had fluid around them. When the blood test came back, a doctor I'd never met sat at the foot of my bed.

"Jeanne," he said, "we need to deliver these babies in the next fifteen minutes. We're going to get an epidural in, then we're going to get them out. You have HELLP syndrome. Your liver is failing."

It was the third, most serious, and final stage after eclampsia. Keith quickly signed a bunch of forms, and they took him with me to the OR. They cut my uterus open, and in the urgent rush to get them out, they cut my bladder too. The doctor pulled out Ezley.

"We have Baby A!" he said. At first, she wasn't breathing. They put an oxygen mask on her and whisked her away. I was trying to stay focused despite the fear overcoming me.

Less than a minute later, he pulled out Xonya.

"Baby B! We have a blonde! We have a blonde!"

Ezley looked like we had imagined based on prior experiences with biracial children, she had big brown eyes, soft olive skin, and her dad's dimple. As evidenced by the doctor's reaction, Xonya was a surprise. She had strawberry blonde hair with bright blue eyes and pink skin.

I was admitted to the ICU where the doctors pumped me with magnesium, and I was monitored very closely for twenty-four hours straight. I wasn't allowed to go see the girls until I could blow into a device that measures lung capacity to prove that the water around my lungs had subsided. They wouldn't let me drink anything either; I was desperately thirsty. I remember my sister letting me put my parched lips on a washcloth. Exactly twenty-four hours after they were born, and after what felt like weeks, I finally got to meet my girls.

CHAPTER 5
BEING BIRACIAL IN AMERICA

WHEN THINKING ABOUT HOW MY PRIVILEGE is different as the wife of a black man, stepmother of a black son, and mother of three biracial children, I find myself aware, not out of empathy—like when growing up and learning about other cultures—but from being exposed to and acutely aware of the privileges I've lost. I share this both shamefully and transparently. It comes from my own experiences, which serve a unique duality of purpose, continually reinforcing my white privilege and amplifying the lack thereof for my black family and loved ones.

As a simple example, take my experience shopping for a doll for my child. I cannot go to a store, any store, and find a doll that looks like Xonya. Do you know where they carry the blue-eyed doll with a blonde afro? If so, where were you on Black Friday 2013 when I was searching?

Although twins, Ezley and Xonya are physically different in so many ways. Xonya has light skin, and Ezley's is darker. Xonya has blue eyes and dark blonde, very curly hair, while Ezley has brown eyes and very thin, soft brown curls. The girls started questioning their ethnicity at an early age. They wondered why only Xonya looked like their cousins on their mom's side. Ezley didn't feel like she looked like any of her relatives, except for her brother, who has the same complexion. One day, Ezley came home from school asking why she wasn't in ESL (English as a Second Language) classes, after classmates had assumed she was Hispanic.

Of course, even young children of color who aren't in Ezley and Xonya's unique situation watch how others are treated. In *Biased: Uncovering the Hidden Prejudice That Shapes What We See, Think, and Do,* author Jennifer L. Eberhardt shares a surprising conversation she had with her then-six-year-old black son, Ebbie, at Thanksgiving: "Out of the blue, he asked, 'Mommy, do you think people see black people as different from white people?'" Eberhardt asked her son leading questions, to which he shared about seeing a black man having an "invisible force field" around him during a recent shopping trip, and that "people kind of stayed away from him a little bit." Eberhardt asked Ebbie what he thought caused that scenario. He gave it some thought. Eberhardt continues, "Just as I was sliding the turkey into the oven, he said in a voice deeper than I had ever heard him use before, 'I think it's fear.'"[20]

While Eberhardt was at first surprised by her son's acuity, she then realized, "That is basically their job, to make connections and to see correlations... They watch us, how we move through the world, to make a determination about how we feel about each other, how we see our own social standing, how we evaluate others" (36–38).

During Quincy's first year of college, he began to embrace his blackness in a new way. He was never ashamed of his ethnicity—that I knew of—but he felt burdened by the history and stigma of slavery. He saw the way his darker peers were treated in relation to himself. In college at UNL, he found himself thrust into his identity, as only 3 percent of the student body is black. Instead of shying away, he embraced it. In addition to taking an African American history class (albeit from a white professor) he grew his hair out into twists during winter break as a way of connecting to his identity and culture. However, this change didn't come without some fear on his part. He asked me if a professor could give him a lower grade because of his hair, if he would get profiled more while driving and if, when returning to work at the golf course after break, he would be sent home for an "unkept" appearance.

Quincy's fears were, of course, not unfounded. My own father had transparently shared with Quincy his bias that he grew to acknowledge. We were at my sister's house for that conversation, celebrating her son's college graduation. My father hadn't seen Q in a while and commented on the length of his twists. Then he told Quincy about going to a wedding of one of his former Boys Town kids. He had been one of the only white people there, and many men had their hair in braids or dreads. He was able to engage in conversation with these men, who did not fit the stereotype he had formed in his head. My father told Quincy he was glad he was being true to himself. It was an important moment for my father, overcoming some of the unconscious biases that had seeped their way into his consciousness.

In addition to constantly comparing and competing with each other, as most siblings do, our biracial children will have to navigate a unique dynamic that only other biracial individuals can understand and relate to. I'm grateful that my children are growing up in a time period in which biracial people are really coming to the forefront, for they will not be alone in their experiences.

One day, Ezley came home from school and shared with Keith what she learned that day. It was Black History Month, and the topic of segregation and Jim Crow laws was discussed in class, including the water fountains that had Whites Only signs. She told Keith that she would not be able to drink from the white one, but her twin sister would. I did not know how to respond to this when he shared it with me; my heart hurt. Yet, here was a teachable moment for our girls, one in which his response would have the potential to shape their identity. Keith let Ezley know, candidly, that Xonya would not have been able to drink from that water fountain. He went on to explain in a way a second grader could understand, whether light or dark skin, in America in the '60s she would have been subject to the same civil rights violations as her sister. Our twins, at this young age, are already experiencing differences that will be embedded deep in their psyche and ultimately will play a role in solidifying the observations that lead to their personal identities. These conversations will undoubtedly continue as we help our girls navigate the present day, persistent systemic racism.

A common worry for parents, and especially those with addiction in the family, is that your child will develop a drug habit. I grew up believing if I were confronted with addiction, I would be supported, not criminalized, and sent with love to a rehab facility to overcome it. The black community has a different and very real experience with addiction; it is not treated as a mental health issue, but rather oftentimes it is met with the most severe of criminal penalties. This difference in treatment is a catalyst for long-term outcomes that have disadvantaged minorities for generations.

My first experience with sending a child off to college is likely different from that of most parents. I would suspect most primarily worry about too much partying and not enough studying. Yes, I worry about these things too, but I also have to worry about my child being targeted by the white supremist on campus whom the university determined was "expressing political views," even though he was threatening violence and packing an automatic weapon. This is the more obvious threat.

Xonya and Ezley will move through life with their own privileges and hardships—both together and individually. Ezley will not be mistaken for white, while Xonya most likely already has. Recently at the grocery store, when it was just Xonya and me, a white cashier commented on her appearance. It was one of the first times we had straightened her hair. "I looked just like her when I was a little girl," she said. "My hair was thick like that too."

Hair realities are much different for the girls, and especially different as twins. Our family was recently planning a trip to a local pumpkin patch for a bonfire and hayrack ride to honor the sixteenth anniversary of my mother's passing. I typically love to seize opportunities to honor her in any way I can, but I contemplated whether we should join our family on this night. I thought, *Do I go, or do I pass, because Xonya will then have to go to school the next day with dirty hair?* My sister can take her daughter and have her hang out by the campfire, get home at 9:00 p.m. and still have time to wash the smoke and hay out of her hair to be ready to roll on Monday morning. I wondered what I could to do to get the smoke out of Xonya's hair that night. I wouldn't be able to wash it, because that would mean I'd keep her up until 1:00 a.m. on a school night. We did end up going, and I covered her head fully with a scarf and hat to minimize the smoke. When we got home, I brushed her hair out and added some conditioner. It worked out for the best, but it is just one of the small things that we must consider that others may not even be aware of.

I'm raising Xonya to be proud of her blackness, and I highly doubt she will purposefully pass for white. Passing is defined as pretending not to be black or part black, which light-skinned, mixed-race women at times did during slavery and abolition for survival. However, she can't help but be "white passing," which means she appears white until she tells the gazer otherwise. Colorism—racism based on skin tone—won't hit her as hard as it will for some biracial children. In fact, with the rising number of interracial children in the United States, her look makes up, according to a May 2019 *Psychology Today* article, one of the most favored mixtures: tan skin and wavy hair, with social media suggesting the "exoticness" of biracial features is to be celebrated, such as the reaction to the light eyes of "hot felon" Jeremy Meeks.[21]

What is so ironic about this celebrated mixture is the reality of the genetics behind it. While taking a class for my master's degree at North Central College in Naperville, Illinois—and while pregnant with Quincy—the class covered a topic about recessive genes. The professor broke down the probability of having X- or Y-colored eyes based on the presence, or lack thereof, of recessive genes. The facts were compelling to me. In order for the son I was carrying to be born with blue or green eyes, his father would have to be carrying a recessive gene. I was aware of the light-skinned ancestors Quincy had, including a paternal-side grandmother with light eyes. With both Quincy and Xonya, this "intriguing" eye color would not have been possible without the recessive genes that, in most cases, came from rape. This is such an important topic to not ignore or minimize. There have been recent attempts from the DNA companies to glamorize the Caucasian and African American gene combination. As tempting as it is to try to rewrite history and create the idea of love affairs between female African American slaves and European American men, in reality there are likely very, very, very few instances in which procreation was the result of a consensual encounter. Just as consent is impossible when someone is drugged or otherwise incapacitated, the simple fact that a female slave was "owned" by her "master" makes consent impossible or improbable at best.

A slave who gave birth to a mixed child would be at risk of suffering the wrath of the slave owner's wife, which included potentially being murdered, as the law would be on the wife's side. *Vox* published an article that states, "[R]ape of black women by white enslavers was so prevalent that a 2016 study revealed 16.7 percent of African Americans' ancestors can be traced back to Europe."[22] Keith, being 9 percent European, is a perfect example of this. When I tell my family that my green-eyed son and blue-eyed daughter have these features as a result of slave rape, I've witnessed their reluctance to accept the reality of the country's past. They love their nephew and niece, and this is a tough and sobering reality to embrace. Keith's DNA analysis clearly shows the introduction of the recessive European gene in the mid-1850s. His family has done an outstanding job of both verbally handing down and documenting their family history, and it is safe to assume there is no slave owner/slave love story; his ancestors were documented slaves at this time. Each time a stranger compliments me on my children's beautiful eyes, it is an opportunity to educate them on this reality.

What does it mean to be biracial in America? I have asked myself this question repeatedly, as a white mother trying to do the best I can to prepare my children for what to expect, without having any true personal insight that I can pass down. For both Keith and me, it has been a struggle to help our biracial children navigate situations that are unique to them, as we are not able to say, "I understand." Neither of us will ever be able to, really.

As I began the process of writing down my thoughts and experiences with raising my children, more often than not, the key challenges I was facing were not "black and white." There were few resources to which I could turn to help navigate the uniqueness of living as two races with two distinct cultures within one family. There are certainly resources available on such topics as "helping a child build confidence," "monitoring the internet," and addressing one culture or another. But mixed cultures? Not so much. And even more so, as I continue to monitor new data and studies that are measuring improvements (or lack thereof), they are "black and white." Where will my kids fall? Must I assume they are always classified as black when it comes to statistics? Does the white data apply to them? Does either set of data apply to them?

Jeanne Jones

How do you help your children have the same appreciation for their European heritage—I want them to be proud of this side of the family too—while also being clear about privilege and the unique opportunity that they will carry throughout their lives to help blend races together by focusing on the many, many ways we are the same and not different?

It is my belief, as a mother to biracial children, that it is my responsibility to aggressively seek to learn all that I can about race relations and social justice in America. These topics have affirmed to me the power behind the social construct of race that has been engineered.

When Quincy was a little boy, there were rarely children's books, movies, or TV shows that were relatable for him. Books and videos centered around white characters, with a token black kid (not biracial) here and there, but that child was never at the center of the story. This is something that I believe white people have to really, really take a step back on and be honest about to appreciate the impact that it has on children of non-white races. Of course, it is important to note that there is a similar impact for children who are LGBTQ+ or have another completely different experience that is exceptionally difficult to navigate and is not represented in mainstream media.

There have been several discussions in which I shared the efforts I took to make sure our kids were enrolled in the most diverse schools possible. Considering we live in a majority white conservative state with few truly diverse public schools, this was important to me. In the end, I chose Burke High School, with 49 percent minority enrollment, with blacks representing the largest of this percentage. This contrasts with the average rate of 4.7 percent for the state.

Typically, when sharing my intentions to ensure my children are in a diverse school, these conversations have led to comments like, "Oh the school is way more diverse than when we were there. I see black kids all the time when I'm picking the kids up," and "Look at the sports teams, they have 'lots' of black kids." It is so interesting to think about this perception. It is easy for white people to feel there is diversity when there are literally just one or two individuals of color in a room full of people. My former high school that was referenced as "being more diverse now" has a black student population of 4 percent, with a total minority population of just 24 percent, 9 percent of which is Asian. For this example, the Asian demographic will not be considered, recognizing that the racial stereotypes for Asians are typically very different and not associated with crime, poverty, lack of education, and some of the other negative stereotypes unique to black and brown people in America, also acknowledging they face their own prejudices and hardships.

If you combine my former high school's black and brown population (including Hispanic and biracial), it is 13 percent. Thirteen percent, meaning only 13 in every 100 students are "like them." When they are in an auditorium, 87 of every 100 people in the room will not be able to relate to their unique experiences being black and brown in America. I would like to challenge non-minorities to see the 1 black person in 10 and qualify how this is diverse. Having been in many situations where I am the only, or one of the only, white people in a room of black or other minorities, I can confidently say that being the 1 in 10 is a much, much different feeling than sitting in a room where 9 of 10 people are like you. It requires intention to not rationalize when a population is under-represented, but rather to embrace it as an opportunity to seek to understand and have the courage to call it what it is: under-representation. And why does representation matter? In a 2012 CNN series, *Kids On Race: The Hidden Picture*, which was aimed at studying children's attitudes on race and understanding how and why they form their opinions, their conclusion speaks to the importance of representation:

> The racial balance of a school can make a major positive difference on how white kids view race. The study tested kids for majority white, majority black and racially mixed schools. The difference was remarkable. Students at majority white schools were the most pessimistic about race. Only 47 percent of kids think their parents would approve of kids from different races being friends. In racially diverse and majority black schools, 71 percent are positive about it. The reason, according to Dr. Killen, is friendship.[23]

To further the point about Asians having a different diversity experience and "classification" from blacks in America, we can simply consider Quincy's experiences throughout junior high and high school.

Quincy was in seventh grade when he began to receive invitations to attend luncheons for programs and other educational and scholarship opportunities for black students. After several of these events—and in doing some research after taking an interest in one of the summer college-bound programs—we learned that these programs were available only to students who were either classified as underserved and living below the poverty line or to those who would be first-generation college students. There was no screening process to ensure that they weren't offering programs to a student who was not an underserved or first-generation college student, thus taking away from a student in need. Basically this told me that every black student at the school was assumed to be underserved. After being selected to attend an expensive invitation-only luncheon for potential scholarship recipients, I wrote to the school trying to help them understand these opportunities should only go to deserving students who would be qualified to take advantage of them.

After Quincy made his decision to not continue with football, we began to discuss the possibility of his transferring to another school where he would be able to meet his highest academic potential. One of the schools we considered was known to have a waitlist for kids who were not living in the district. I decided to do some research to better understand if there were efforts to promote diversity at the school, with the hope that he may bypass the waiting list if this was the case. I was thrilled when I located the district bylaws online, and they confirmed what I had hoped. The wording of the bylaw was something to the effect of: "to contribute to the diversity of the school, African American students will not be required to be on a waiting list." I shared the good news with Quincy and let him know that I was going to call the school to arrange a tour and get him registered.

"Hello." I was confident the school administrator could sense the excitement in my voice. "We are considering transferring our son, and I would love to set up time for him to take a tour of the school. I have done some research and learned that African American students do not have to be on the waiting list; he is African American."

"Oh, that that is wonderful," the woman replied. "And you are correct, he would not need to be put on the waiting list. I'm just going to need you to email me the documentation that you would have filled out for the free lunch program."

"He is not on the free lunch program. We will not be needing that," I responded.

There was quite a pause as she was thinking through this. "Well in that case, he is going to have to be on the waiting list."

"I'm not sure I understand. I have the bylaw right here in front of me, I did my research, and it indicates that African American students can bypass the waitlist to promote diversity," I explained. I'm sure she could sense how annoyed I was.

"It may say that, but what it *means* is that we allow those students who qualify for the free lunch program to bypass the waiting list," she replied.

"But that is *not* what the bylaw states," I repeated. This time the pause was on my part. I knew I needed to help her understand what was happening here. "If it is required to be on the free lunch program in order to bypass the waiting list, your bylaw implies you *assume that every African American student is underserved and will qualify?*"

"Well I assure you that is not the intent," she explained.

"I understand that, but I assure you that that is exactly what it implies. I understand that you are not responsible for this and you simply follow the rules, not create them. Please pass on that I will be writing to the board of directors and I will do everything I can to ensure this is changed," I said.

Quincy did not transfer to this district for this reason. I did follow up sometime later to see if there had been an amendment to the bylaw, and there had been one. In the section for student enrollment priorities, it now reads "students…who contribute to the socioeconomic diversity of enrollment can bypass the waitlist for enrollment." One small step forward.

When I was pregnant with Quincy, I spent almost every night reading the book *What to Expect When You're Expecting.* I wanted to know everything, good, bad, and ugly regarding what to expect throughout my pregnancy and what to expect during the first year of his life.

One of the things the book forgot to mention was that if you are having a biracial child, after they are born you should expect people to ask you if they are adopted, or they may just assume they are adopted, and begin asking you questions about your "experience with adoption." This is something I had not thought about nor prepared for. The mention of adoption is not in any way intended to take away from the selfless decision and courageous act of kindness for those who give up a child or adopt. I have the utmost respect and appreciation for anyone who has participated in this process, and in fact Keith and I had taken adoption classes together before the girls were born in anticipation of someday being adoptive parents ourselves.

When Q was around seven months old, I had to take him in to the doctor for one of the many viral infections that he experienced in the early months of his daycare experience. The nurse who was checking us in began to do her intake questions.

"So this is Quincy?" she asked.

"Yes!" I replied.

"And he is seven months old?" she asked.

"Yes." Wow these were easy questions.

"And you're his…?" she asked.

"Excuse me?" This one I didn't quite understand. I looked at her quizzically.

"You're his...?" she repeated.

I still was not getting it, so I just looked at her with a blank stare.

"Are you his nanny?" she asked.

Okay, now I understood.

"No? No, I'm his mom?" I had an inflection in my response. More so because I was seeking an explanation for her line of questioning. I wanted her to tell me why in the world she would question who I was. I didn't get a response.

"I gave birth to him. He is my son." I left it at that.

As Q got a little older, in his toddler years, he began wearing an afro. I think this may have thrown people off, considering many mixed kids have curly hair but cannot always pull off an afro. Quincy's was unique in that he had lighter brown hair with blonde highlights on each side above his eyes. It was during this time when I took him with me to the mall in Kansas City. For some reason, that day there were clowns walking around the mall. Quincy spotted one as I was leaving a store, and it sent him into a frenzy. He began screaming, saying "Help me!" at the top of his lungs. I rushed to get him out of the mall, or at least out of view of the clown. A security guard spotted me and began following me at a distance. I heard him on his radio, "I'm going to need backup, this woman is carrying a child that is screaming *help*. It is *not* hers," he said. "This is not her child," he repeated with urgency in his voice.

I whipped around and started walking toward him to confront the situation head on. I asked quite calmly under the circumstances if he could please help me calm my son down by getting us away from the clown.

"Ma'am, I'm going to need to detain you until I can make sure this is your son," he explained.

Luckily, Quincy's daycare had made all of the parents' cards with their kids' pictures and fingerprints on them. I sure was happy this day to have this on me. Once I showed him the card, the security guard apologized. I understood the need to validate this was my child under the circumstances; after all, Quincy was yelling, "Help!" Two decades later and with the biracial population exploding, I don't believe as many parents will have this same experience. But I still question, if I were carrying a little boy who looked like me, would I have needed to explain my son was frantic because he was afraid of a clown? It is likely I would have been met with help, not questioned.

You can imagine the looks that Keith would get when he used to stroll around our twin girls. He has been a stay-at-home dad since they were born, and he would often take them to the mall in the morning to walk. At the time, Ezley had soft straight hair and resembled Dora from *Dora the Explorer*; Xonya was nicknamed Pinky for her light pink skin and strawberry blonde curls. We would joke about the elderly couples and walking club members thinking he was a daddy daycare situation; they must've thought they couldn't possibly both be his. Joking about it is pretty much the most important thing to do, we have learned over time—just take it in stride. When regularly asked at Target, a restaurant, and the grocery store if your kids are adopted, the best response is to just smile and say, "Nope." For fun, I like to throw in that the girls are twins, which is typically met with an incredulous, "No?"

Jeanne Jones

It's going to be a challenge to raise both my girls with full confidence about their places in the world. Luckily, the rise in interracial children has changed the perception of what it means to be American in many parts of the United States. They will see themselves reflected in TV shows, media, and sports, such as soccer, golf, and swimming, more than Quincy did, and their school is even more diverse now than when he attended.

And as the multiracial population grows, so will the many, many combinations the genetics pool offers. A *Washington Post* article reveals that from 2010 (the year the girls were born) to 2015, those who identified as being part of two or more races grew by *24 percent.*

Additionally, the Pew Research Center provides some detailed analytics:

- Between 2000 and 2010, the number of white and black biracial Americans more than doubled.

- The racial background of the largest group of multiracial babies (36 percent) is black and white.

- 1 in 7 U.S. infants (14 percent) were multiracial or multiethnic in 2015—nearly triple the share in 1980.

- In 1980, 7 percent of all newlyweds were in an interracial marriage; by 2015 that share had more than doubled to 17 percent.[24]

While I celebrate the rise in ethnic diversity—especially when considering the world I want my children to live in—I know that the multiracial community will not save America from its deep-seated racism, nor should it be asked to. Historically, other ethnicities who did not fit into the White Anglo-Saxon Protestant (WASP) mold were able to assimilate into "whiteness" over a short generational period. The Irish and Italians, for example, have phenotypes and features not far removed from the depiction of whiteness, and in just one generation, a child of a WASP and an Irishman or Italian could "fit in." For black Americans, on the other hand, assimilation has not occurred at such a rate. Black features and skin tone differ from whiteness at a larger degree, making it more difficult for their mixed-race offspring to blend in. I say this crudely, because it *is* crude. If America doesn't rescind its engrained penchant for seeing "color" on a good/bad spectrum, which it engineered, a mixed-race country will not cure racism. For example, in a popular NPR article called "Why Mixed-Race Americans Will Not Save the Country," Alexandros Orphanides writes, "The fact that mixed-race people who present as non-white face discrimination because of their proximity to a non-white group reinforces the idea of racial discrimination emphasizing categorization with one group, rather than hybridity."[25]

I wonder how familiar most white people are with the term *colorism*. What a complex thing it is; so many people experience it on a regular basis, but, similar to unconscious bias, they do not realize it is all around them. White people can even perpetuate it without knowing they're doing so. Many mixed-race men and women hear such "compliments" from whites as: "You're not what I typically think of when I see a man with dreads." "You're not like other black people I've met." "I see you as just white like me." "You have an exotic look." "You speak so well."

Jeanne Jones

I can only imagine how much of this Quincy has experienced growing up, and how much my girls will experience as they get older. It is not intentionally biased, but it is stemming from implicit bias. This makes it all that much more important for people to be educated and aware of it, because it does have consequences. For example, between the ages of seven and ten, Quincy did some modeling and a TV commercial for a large cable provider. He was nicknamed the One-Shot Wonder by one of the major marketing companies that was using him for print ads; modeling seemed to come naturally to him. As opportunities continued to roll in, and his experience grew, he became less and less interested. By ten years old, he decided he wanted to "retire" from modeling, suggesting that he wanted to focus on football instead. We fully supported him; it was his decision. Years later, we learned his motivation for wanting to leave a promising opportunity that he was doing well with was that, "it was just one more thing making me feel different." And it was in fact his "different" and "exotic" look that was being recruited and highlighted during each of these photo shoots. I didn't connect it then with colorism, but I do now.

At times I wonder, given Xonya and Ezley's different appearances, how much the "compliments" will vary. For me, even before I had my children, colorism was very evident in the arts and entertainment. When you think about the early African American actresses who were breaking the color barriers, who do you think of? What do they have in common? Most actresses until quite recently have been lighter skinned with less ethnic features. This, of course, perpetuates and results from colonial influence.

Colorism has been involved in the fabric of our country since its inception. It's well documented that lighter-skinned female slaves were often "house slaves," while those with darker skin worked in the fields. This disparity resulted from slave owners giving "privileges" to slaves who had been born as a result of rape from a white slave owner. They were often deemed more trustworthy, because of both their lineage and their more European appearance. Those who created them could pat themselves on the back for giving their secret progeny a "better life" than the rest of the slaves—while still enslaving them. Historian Obiora N. Anekwe has said, "In order to become an effective slave owner, Willie Lynch [where the term *lynching* comes from] argued that 'you must use the dark skin slaves vs. the light skin slaves, and the light skin slaves vs. the dark skin slaves... They must love, respect and trust only us... The slaves themselves will remain perpetually distrustful of each other.'"[26]

Horribly, Lynch's plan worked. Anekwe went on to say, "This system of color segregation helped establish and promote what we now know as colorism within the international black community." The community uses terms to describe each other based on appearance, and almost all of the terms are meant as insults meant to create a barrier between the speaker and receiver—such insults as redbone, high yellow, darkie, blackie, blackard, whitewash, and "light, bright, and almost white."

Back in the nineteenth and twentieth centuries, some black communities even used what's referred to as the Brown Paper Bag Test, wherein only those who were the same shade or lighter than a paper bag were allowed entry. Some have dismissed this test as urban legend, but its existence is asserted by historian Henry Louis Gates, Jr. in his book *The Future of Race*. He notes that he learned of "bag parties" from Yale classmates who hailed from New Orleans. Those who used the test sadly knew that white Americans would be more tolerant of them than of their darker-skinned brothers and sisters. Case in point, the National Conference for Community and Justice states, "Women with light skin served 11 percent less time in prison than darker women…[and]…light-skinned women were sentenced to approximately 12 percent less time behind bars than their darker-skinned counter parts."[27]

As someone with white privilege, the topic of colorism is not something I bring up to judge or criticize the black community. Rather, it's indicative of just how strong color-based racism was and is in Eurocentric American culture; not talking about it will not serve us well if we want to move to a better place for our next generations—a place of education, a place of understanding.

My biracial children will benefit from colorism in varying degrees. It would be naive for me to believe that each of my children will have the same experiences, simply because they all came from or were raised with me. Rather, colorism is ingrained not just in our culture but in cultures the world over, including in the official caste system of India and the unofficial caste system of Brazil. Even this can be traced back to Lynch. Anekwe said, "As Willie Lynch's message of dividing and conquering black enslaved people spread throughout North America, it also gained acceptance as an effective means to guarantee the enslavement of other colonized people around the world."[28]

Many black American women are recognizing the pitfalls of holding onto the persistent colonial definitions of beauty and demarcation and are banding together against it. Kiri Laurelle

Davis, a filmmaker and media consultant, recently said in an interview, "solidarity between Black women of varying skins tones looks and feels like a sisterhood—a sisterhood that strives to be supportive, consisting of understanding and mutual respect. Although unified, it also allows us space to acknowledge and embrace that our experiences differ, and that that is okay."[29] Just as other countries attempt to divide Americans for their own gain, white Americans divide African Americans through the perpetuation of colorism.

CHAPTER 6
RACE RELATIONS

FOR BOTH THE 2008 AND 2012 presidential election results, I was in our living room sipping on a Bacardi and Diet Coke to ease my anxiousness. In 2008, our country stood at a crossroads that could make history. Had we come far enough to elect our first black president, not to mention, one with a Muslim name and a father who was an immigrant? When the 2008 results were called for Barack Obama, I dropped to my knees and wept. A dizziness came over me, and I felt as though I was having an out-of-body experience. My mind raced, thinking about what it meant to my young black son, who happened to be biracial like our newly elected president, and my stepson, both of whom will navigate life as black men. The limits for them that I had created in my mind—while resisting them every step of the way, but also challenging myself to be eyes-wide-open to the lack of progress and the data that validated these thoughts—seemed to subside. We turned on old-school music and danced around, soaking in the moment. I was so hopeful about the future. The future became *now*, and I instantly believed they could be anything. I marveled at what equal opportunity would look like five years into the future.

I had no idea how the next eight years would unfold. I especially had no idea how deep and wide the blood pumping through the veins of superiority ran. Of course, after eight years of utter resistance and a ground swell of hypocrisy, we're now living in the regression of that unprecedented progress. While it's maddening, and even terrifying, it speaks to the nation's fear of losing its identity—even a fabricated one.

In storybooks, in school, and in song, America was founded on the belief that good, hardworking men will be rewarded with—and are even due—wealth and expanse. However, in order to accumulate both, free labor was necessary.

Slavery started before Columbus came to America, but in America it became a fine-tuned machine. In *Stamped from the Beginning: The Definitive History of Racist Ideas in America*, author Ibram X. Kendi wrote that the term *slave* originated from *Slav*, as Slavs made up the largest group of Eastern European slaves in Western Europe. By the mid-1400s, the Slavs had built up a fortress that largely protected them from capture, and Africans became the new slaves. It was then that slavery was first associated with blackness. There are many misconceptions about Irish "slaves" in the United States and of Africans enslaving their own people. While servitude has taken place in many regions, an article in *Slate* magazine states that it was Africans, and then, through procreation, black Americans, who were actual, chattel slaves.[30] Thus, the history of American wealth was built on the literal backs of an enslaved people.[31]

This sordid history is now acknowledged but often downplayed. Many surmise, "If I didn't own slaves, how can I be at fault? Slavery was so long ago." In actuality, American slavery ended less than 200 years ago. The Spanish began to enslave Native Americans almost immediately after immigrating to America with Christopher Columbus in 1492. In 1516, due to a decreased Native American labor force, the case was made to bring enslaved Africans to the country, and in 1619 the first Africans arrived after a Portuguese slave ship was seized by the English. The Portuguese, for their part, had been major players in England's slave trade since the mid-1400s.

Even when slavery ended in 1865, blacks were not allowed to own property (thus, the significance of Keith's ancestors being sharecroppers to a black landowner). It would be about fifty more years before blacks could vote. Interracial marriage (specifically, marriage between a white and non-white individual) was not made constitutionally legal until June 12, 1967, when Mildred and Richard Loving successfully took on the State of Virginia. Our biracial twins were, poetically, born exactly forty-three years later on June 12, 2010, my late mother's birthday, which is now referred to as Loving Day. While it was unenforceable after 1967, Alabama kept its anti-miscegenation (anti-interracial relationship) ban until the year 2000, as a "symbolic statement" of the state's views.

I experienced this sentiment firsthand on a trip to the South for a family reunion in the mid-1990s. I was one of only two white family members in a very large group. While at a restaurant, we were asked to wait well over an hour as the management repeatedly and almost immediately sat large groups without reservations coming in behind us. There were plenty of open tables, and it was obvious we could have been easily accommodated, but instead we sat and patiently waited. We were eventually seated in a back room of the restaurant. After getting up to take my biracial nephews to the restroom, who were just toddlers at the time, I was sneered at and verbally assaulted, with someone calling us "disgusting."

With every advancement in equality, a large part of the population attempted to—and often succeeded in—blocking their efforts, whether through scare tactics or unreasonable new "rules." The Ku Klux Klan was first formed in 1867, as a fear response to the newly freed slaves during Southern Reconstruction. The second wave took place during World War I, when a large number of Southern blacks relocated—in what was called The Great Migration—to the newly industrialized American Midwest. Race-based Supreme Court rulings in the 1950s brought on the third wave, which kept pace with the burgeoning Civil Rights Movement. It's safe to say that we are now in the fourth wave.

Each of the KKK's surges happened as a fear response to change, according to an article in *JSTOR Daily*. Fear causes actions, which cause suffering, which causes fear.[32] In terms of communities, this fear is based on in-groups versus out-groups— alliances that promote identity but also shut out others, and they are often more malleable than we think, changing based on whatever is most convenient for the in-group. For example, the United States census has altered its racial designations for centuries. The first designation, in 1790, listed *Free white males [and] females*, *All other free persons*, and *Slaves*. In 1820, *All other free persons* changed to *Free colored males and females*. In 1850, a "racial scientist" added *mulatto* (mixed-race person) to see "if there was any kind of drop-off in their lifespan," as "blacks and whites may have been different species." In 1890, *mulatto* was expanded

Jeanne Jones

to differentiate between *quadroons* and *octoroons*—those who were one-fourth and one-eighth black, respectively. Then in 1930, all were replaced with *Negro*.[33]

In 1968, the day after the assassination of Martin Luther King Jr., third-grade teacher Jane Elliot tried an exercise to teach her white, rural Iowan students about discrimination, and how easy it is to "out-group" people. In the Blue Eyes and Brown Eyes Experiment, which later became nationally recognized, she separated her students by eye color. The first day, she told her students that brown-eyed people were superior. The brown-eyed children took to the discrimination almost immediately, and she watched the power dynamics unfold before her eyes. The second day, she switched the superiority to those with blue eyes, and the children once again responded in an intense in-group/out-group fashion.[34]

In season three of the TV comedy *The Good Place*, the mixed-race, social scientist Simone tries to educate the self-centered, white Eleanor about the natural stages people go through as they evolve into thoughtful human beings:

> As humans evolve, the first big problem we had to overcome was "me versus us." Learning to sacrifice a little individual freedom for the benefit of the group. You know, like sharing food and resources so we don't starve and get eaten by tigers. The next problem to overcome was "us versus them." Trying to see other groups different from ours as equals. That one we're still struggling with.

Comically, Simone tells Eleanor she hasn't passed the first stage. Simone sees those who hold onto racist and nationalist beliefs as not overcoming the "us versus them" stage. To quote Vietnamese Buddhist monk Thich Nhat Hanh, "We are here to awaken from the illusion of our separateness." What divides us isn't as big as we think. We are more alike than we are different, and "awakening" to this reality helps us walk in others' shoes and see a larger picture.

Our country is at a critical stage of its development, in which the 1 percent (those who control the top 1 percent of wealth in the nation) are once again responding and working to pit us against one another through fear tactics. Each group (including the 1 percent) fears that it will lose some fundamental part of its identity, or some right to existence on which its life and livelihood depend. Groups can become so blinded by their own fear of annihilation that they don't see they're working to annihilate others. This is history repeating itself again—the Trail of Tears, the Holocaust, Darfur, Japanese internment camps, and not to be made light of, the deployment of the national guard and the use of excessive force at peaceful protests. Our nation is currently dehumanizing brown-skinned immigrants—especially those coming through the U.S.–Mexico border, with the border wall and through Executive Order 13769, referred to as the Muslim Travel Ban, with a growing list of countries being denied entrance.

I often ask Q questions to try to gauge his level of awareness of current events and changes that are taking place. At this young adult age, it takes interest and effort to pay attention to what is happening around him and to be able to put it into historical perspective, especially when history has not been well documented when it comes to responses. We were out to dinner for Keith's birthday when I posed my usual question, "Are you paying attention to what is going on around you?" Quincy responded that he was taking a class called Black Experience in Politics led by family friend and local Black Votes Matter founder Preston Love, Jr. Preston served as Jesse Jackson's presidential campaign manager, among his many other honorable civic duties, and I was excited to hear he would be teaching Q about his firsthand experiences with civil rights.

Along the lines of implicit bias (what is taught) is the way our education system minimizes and glosses over the cruelty of slavery, the intentional and racist practices of Jim Crow laws and disparities in social justice (what is *not* taught). The Civil Rights Movement is frequently taught as emerging from and catapulted by Rosa Parks who would not give up her seat on a bus one random day. There is little mention of the social research, strategic planning, and coordination that took place for *years* prior to this one event. Parks not giving up her seat that day was not random, it was a well-planned, well-timed, and well-coordinated event. In a similar vein, in elementary schools the Civil Rights Movement is almost singularly taught as being practiced by Dr. Martin Luther King Jr., instead of a movement of the people across our country that when unraveled would show a long and complex web of events and individual acts of courage that are invisible in our history books. This is not to minimize the brilliance and charisma of Dr. King, but there were so many unsung heroes in the throes with him that are regularly overlooked. The danger is that the singular focus diminishes the message to young students that they can be inspired by one of many, many people who looked like them who were smart, courageous, and made a difference. Focusing on one person presents the movement as requiring just one person to rise from the ashes to make a difference, instead of the possibility of everyday heroes surrounding us and enacting positive change. My hope for my children is that there will be a growing willingness by the masses to seek to understand and this will require embracing a comprehensive historical view.

When Quincy mentioned taking Preston's class, he went on to tell us about responses that occur with each step forward in Democratic progress. We've seen this with an increase in lynchings after the Emancipation Proclamation and in increased violence following the Civil Rights Act of 1964. In the country's most recent, widespread case, the loud voices in our country that are growing increasingly emboldened and racist are a response to the progress our country made in electing its first black president, twice. I challenged Quincy to ponder, "What do the responses mean for you?" Since he has been raised with a level of privilege, I want to make sure he connects the dots and really understands the personal impact the complicity with racism will have on him and his younger brother and sisters. More importantly, I wanted to make sure I got the sense that he understood his responsibility to do his part to advocate for continued change in the face of these disheartening responses.

A couple weeks after the 2016 election, I was in line at Walmart with my twin girls. A large, bearded white man, about 6′6″ and in a leather biker vest, turned around in line to stare us down. He puffed himself up; the hate in his eyes was palpable. I looked around, and there was no other target in sight, this hate was directed at me and the girls. I thought about confronting him, but considering my stature, that thought did not last long.

Instead I grabbed the girls and pulled them close to me as I stared back at him, hoping my locked eyes would communicate that I wasn't afraid, even though I was. All I could think was, *How am I going to explain this to the girls?* They clearly picked up on his encroachment and the ensuing stare down. After we cautiously left the store, I explained to them that he was mad at something and must be an unhappy person. Before the election, I hadn't come across someone this emboldened. Yes, there were definitely the "looks" of disapproval, but they were easy to dismiss and I never felt threatened by them. It is amazing how quickly the hate came out in the open, rising from the shadows.

I have experienced these annoyed and disgusted sentiments multiple times since, and I expect them to continue as the complacency and normalization of racist behavior continues to grow. Unlike when raising Quincy, I am now in the unfortunate position of needing to teach my young girls about being on guard and aware of their surroundings at all times as well as how to recognize signs that someone may be racist. With the boys, I didn't feel I needed to teach this because even if they were confronted with racism, I always felt the people around them would find it intolerable and would step up and do the right thing. I no longer believe this, and instead I am focusing on teaching my children how to practice tolerance, and, in a worst-case scenario, how to physically defend themselves.

As an example of the dangerous shift in allowing hate to be tolerated as a political view or free speech, hate has infected the meaning of the American flag. It has, in many cases, become synonymous with the Make America Great Again movement, or for some, the dog whistle of Make America White Again. When my kids see trucks with the big flags waving, which are a symbol of the drivers' "patriotism," the symbol may also be a warning sign for them to put their guard up and be vigilant about what's going on around them. It is incredibly ironic that a flag meant to unite a country is now often used to make a huge portion of the population feel on edge. When my girls were born, I never, *ever* would have believed for one minute that I would have to teach them about being on guard and to watch for signs of racist behavior when they see an American flag.

I have seen more racially motivated flag flying in the last three years than I did in the first forty-seven years of my life. And they are in my own backyard. Literally. A family in our neighborhood hung a Betsy Ross flag, and a half-confederate half-American flag was hung adjacent to one of our local high schools. On July 27, 2019, the local KMTV Omaha news station reported: "The man responsible for hanging the flag is working on the tower, telling 3 News Now he likes having it up while he works and that it's a representation of culture, not racism. The employee said he hangs the flag on every cell tower he works on." Again, this cannot be normalized or accepted, it is hate and should be addressed as such.

In fact, things have regressed so far that one may not get any signals at all before being killed for no reason. In July 2019, Elijah Al-Amin, a black seventeen-year-old, was stabbed from behind and then slit in the throat in a Circle K convenience store in Peoria, Arizona. His crime? He was listening to rap music while standing beside the soda machine. I have seen countless news stories of the use of swastikas, Confederate flags, racial slurs, and xenophobic cases of vandalism. Keeping my children safe has taken on an entirely new meaning.

Our family has had both positive and negative experiences at restaurants. There have been times I've had to stop Keith from a possible confrontation when we were met with glares, snide comments, and annoyance at our colorful family, one example being when we were at a local breakfast diner on one of my days off work and Kaydon was staying with us so we had the whole family. Across the room from us sat four elderly men who shortly after we sat down began to intentionally raise their voice so we could hear their conversation. They were discussing how intriguing the documentary was that they had watched on Hitler and the Third Reich, and how they are now seeing this historical perspective highlighted more often. It was up to us to translate this: Were they intrigued by the horror of it? Or were they intrigued by the possibility that white supremacy may someday evolve to this level in America? Either way, it was their privilege that enabled them to be comfortable bringing this up at all in front of our family.

Other times, people literally go out of their way to stop by our table to say how "sweet" or "unique" our family is, typically saying things like, "You have a beautiful family." I remember after our third or fourth time experiencing this, we looked at each other and wondered if these individuals recognize that they are differentiating our family because of our varied skin tones, albeit in a kind way with positive intent. In either instance, our simple presence, eating together as a colorful family, stirred emotion they were compelled to act on.

In the months leading up to the November 2016 election, we now know that social media was crawling with Russian-driven posts that promoted conspiracy theories, and closet racists began coming out of the woodwork. With it came a boldness among "friends" to begin to share equally absurd conversations or angry emotions about their disdain for the Obama administration. All of a sudden, it was like there was a bright spotlight on what had been around me for the past eight years, but had previously been hidden and festering in the dark. I already knew that some—what I thought was a very small number—of ignorant people were buying into the "birther" conspiracy early on. What I did not realize was how many intelligent people were already ignoring their logical thought processes and critical-thinking skills to allow their deep-seated fear and uncertainty about having a black president surface. This was a turning point for me.

✳ ✳ ✳

A family member and I were making small talk in the waiting room one day when my sister was in surgery at a local hospital.

"I can't believe Obama hasn't done anything about black-on-black crime in Chicago," he said. "He should be addressing this."

I was dumbfounded. "Why do you think the president of the United States should be the one accountable for a long-standing history of crime happening within a subsection of a larger city? Has any other president addressed this, or would they have been expected to take up such a local issue?"

In hindsight, I really wish I had given him a better response. I have replayed the scene in my head a thousand times, as it was such a missed opportunity to challenge and educate. It dawned on me that those who did not like President Obama were really starting to grasp at straws to come up with character flaws now that his presidency was coming to an end. It felt so odd that he would have the audacity to make this comment to me, as if I were somehow going to find it logical. He had never before been invested in crime in Chicago, and all these years he never took it upon himself to advocate that the president of the United States is responsible for fixing it. He was aware of the root causes associated with crime—including the physical oppression in the building design of the housing projects, poverty, and family dysfunction, yet absurdly was pointing to the president as lacking accountability.

Over the past two years, I've quizzically heard several more elderly white men complain about crime in Chicago; before Obama had taken office, I had never heard any person commenting on the crime in an American city they didn't even live in. After the conversation at the hospital, it became clear that it had nothing to do with crime in Chicago. This was a fear response to a black leader.

Certainly no person who votes for a president who asked for the death penalty for the Central Park Five—and then stood by it after the young men were exonerated—cares about black-on-black crime in Chicago. No person who votes for a president who has settled discrimination lawsuits and calls the far right "fine people"—and predominantly brown and black countries "shitholes"—really cares about black-on-black crime in Chicago.

Recently I picked up donuts on the way to work for a team member's birthday. Two men, whom I assumed were retired, were in the shop. One immediately commented on my car; he was an Audi fan too. I explained I purchased it in Chicago, because the pricing is so much more competitive. (There is only one Audi dealership where I live.) I told the men what a great experience I'd had with it so far, and that I would take advantage of every chance I get to go back to Chicago, where I once lived. As I was leaving, the other man, after clear contemplation and with a sneer on his face, asked, "How did you get it out of Chicago without bullet holes?" I started to reply, and instead just shook my head and gave him a look of disappointment.

When I hear these comments thinly (or not so thinly?) veiled in underlying racism, I find myself still unsure about how to proceed. For one, I was raised to respect my elders, so in this case I didn't feel comfortable calling the man a jackass. In hindsight, I really wish I had, but I always hear Michelle Obama's voice in my head, saying, "When they go low, we go high." Hopefully he read this in my eyes.

Another response has come in the form of conspiracy theory email chains that get splattered around and discussed over morning coffee. The "problem" doesn't impact them at all, but it festers because they are scared. It also "relieves" them of their own complicity in maintaining the status quo, much like the "African-on-African" slavery argument.

I wonder if that same man in the donut shop had been complicit in receiving and believing the conspiracy theory emails that seemed to be making the rounds among older, white men. In February 2019, *USA Today* reported on such email chains to and from billionaire Joe Ricketts that were made public, which had been sent between 2009 and 2013. The article called out that the emails, which included the birtherism conspiracy and Muslim hate, naturally taint the Ricketts family—including son Tom Ricketts, owner of the Chicago Cubs. Tom Ricketts only half-apologized for the content, while being quick to reinforce that his father is in no way associated with the Chicago Cubs organization. However, it was Joe Ricketts and his wife who paid for the purchase. From his same pocket, he also had plans to spend $10 million to fund a smear campaign against Obama before the 2012 election. Chicago's president of the Muslim Community Center, Kamran Hussain, wrote to the Ricketts family and urged them to meet with Muslim Chicagoans. About his love for the Cubs and Joe Ricketts's politics, Hussain said, "I don't think I can keep compartmentalizing those things."[35] It was gracious for Hussain to call Joe Ricketts's beliefs "politics." Just as with the "political views" the UNL white supremacist spouted, this was racism, pure and simple. We are going down a very dangerous road of normalizing hate as political views. This has to change. Call out hate as hate, racism as racism.

Unlike the 2008 and 2012 elections—during which I felt a tidal wave of hope pour over me—the election of 2016 had the opposite effect. Instead of riding a wave, I felt I was drowning. I wept once again, but this time for a very different reason. I wept for my children and for what it would mean to our family.

Shortly after the election was called, I went into the girls' bedroom and just stood in disbelief while I watched them sleeping innocently. I had no idea what I was going to tell them in the morning when they awoke. I had spent the months prior trying to educate them—at their age-appropriate level of understanding—that there was a person running in the election who had exhibited outright racially discriminatory behavior, and that if he were chosen to lead our country, it would be difficult for families like ours. Yet here we were. *How could this happen? How?*

As overwhelming and confusing as it was to accept the results, I took comfort in knowing that our family would not be alone. I also received validation that my thoughts about what the results were telling us—and what they were saying about us as a country—were unfortunately real. Of course, I could not sleep, so I kept watching to hear what the political analysts had to say; I thought maybe they could help me make sense of this. The validation came when I heard Van Jones, nearly in tears, ask the same question that had been reeling in my head: "What am I am going to tell my children tomorrow?"

Over the following months, I was shocked and saddened to learn about friends and family members who had quietly elected someone they knew had not only admitted to sexually assaulting women, committing adultery, openly disparaging military members and war heroes, and mocking the disabled, but who had also repeatedly exhibited racist behaviors and had a well-documented track record to prove it. It was not simply a rumor or conspiracy theory that he may have racist tendencies. There was example after example of him wielding his privilege and of him calling to action all those like him who wanted to keep that privilege. I wondered whether the thought of me and my family—or any other friend or family member who would be so devastatingly impacted—ever entered their minds. How was it possible that they would overlook not only deep, deep character flaws, but something incredibly dangerous to our country? What would compel them to support someone whose behavior was completely unacceptable for the least of our leaders? I learned quickly that I was completely ignorant to the ignorance, complacency, and acceptance that those with privilege had to the struggles of those without.

Jeanne Jones

CONCLUSION
MIXED

THERE ARE SO MANY JOYS that come with being a wife and mother in a mixed-race family. I am so proud of my kids, and as much as I know that I will need to advocate for them to have a place that is equal and accepting, I also feel a heaviness for the responsibility that they will carry to be a voice that can educate and enable bringing two sides together. An article in *Psychology Today* explains the power of this responsibility: "By not fitting neatly into one category...researchers say the growing number of multiracial Americans may help the rest of the population develop the flexibility to see people as more than just a demographic—and to move away from race as a central marker of identity."[36]

The country's two "opposite" races have struggled for years and years, and a unified nation will not be realized until we truly have equality and social justice. To do that will take a movement. And it is not just biracial children—or children of any particular race—who will need to take up this moment, but rather all people, young and old alike, who believe in moving our country forward into an antiracist future. Founding director of the Boston University Center for Antiracist Research Ibram X.

Kendi says, "The most effective protests have been fiercely local; they are protests that have been started by antiracists focusing on their immediate surroundings: their blocks, neighborhoods, schools, colleges, jobs, and professions." Young people make a difference when they realize the power of standing strong right where they are—wherever they find themselves.

The world is learning that it is not enough to just move through life claiming not to be racist, yet not advocating as an antiracist. In Kendi's *How to Be an Antiracist*, he poses the question, "What is the problem with being 'not racist'? It is a claim that signifies neutrality: 'I am not a racist, but neither am I aggressively against racism.' But there is no neutrality in the racism struggle… One either allows racial inequities to persevere, as a racist, or confronts racial inequities, as an antiracist. There is no in-between safe space of 'not racist'. The claim of 'not racist' neutrality is a mask for racism."[37]

We are currently in a time of response to progress that has been made. We must quiet this response and stand firm in the belief that our nation is not one of hate and divisiveness, but one of humanity and hope. In her book's conclusion, Jennifer L. Eberhardt says:

> The mistake we keep making—the mistake we all keep making—is in thinking that our work is done. That whatever heroic effort we've made will keep moving us forward. That whatever progress we've seen will keep us from sliding back to burning crosses … [T]his moment in Charlottesville [Unite the Right Rally] is our lot, our inheritance. This is where our history and our brain machinery strand us—time and time again. Moving

forward requires vigilance. It requires us to constantly attend to who we are, how we got that way and all the selves we have the capacity to be.[38]

The saying "history repeats itself" is so popular because it's *true*. I frequently encourage friends and family to read the book *Ordinary Men* by Christopher Browning with an open mind—and with keeping the many recent, unprecedented hate-based events top of mind. Browning's book is a recounting of Reserve Police Battalion 101 of the German Order Police. This order was responsible for mass shootings and for rounding up Jewish citizens to deport to Poland in 1942. Most Americans picture Nazis as monsters who killed for their own gain, but Browning asserts that the truth is much more disturbing. Most of the RPB 101 were "ordinary middle-aged working-class men who committed these atrocities out of a mixture of motives, including group dynamics of conformity, deference to authority, role adaptation, and the altering of moral norms to justify their actions." Put simply, not all of these men entered into their positions with inherent racist leanings. They allowed themselves to be swayed by in-group dynamics and the casting aside of moral behavior to assuage their fear of losing their country to a perceived out-group.

Does this sound familiar? It should. Recent leaders promoting propaganda have created, sustained, and reinforced fear through the bombardment of false messages. Browning was recently interviewed about these similarities:

What went wrong post–World War I in Germany is instructive, but it is not an exact parallel for what is happening today in America... One thing that is clear, however, is that if people do not accept the ground rules by which democracy operates, and winning at all costs and incivility become the norm, then things fall apart. There has to be an acceptance of the norms and rules, and a sense of obligation to one another and the democracy, by the broader political community. We see that falling apart with political polarization now. And that was true in the 1930s with the rise of authoritarianism and fascism in Europe and elsewhere.

The protests that stemmed from George Floyd's death were the start of a movement, and sweeping changes have been made and continue to be made as a result. All across our country we are now seeing Americans stepping up in a way we have not seen in decades. What this will mean for narrowing the gaps with the many disparities we have as a country remains to be seen. Time will tell.

What is clear is that it is time for us to say good-bye to viewing our nation through the lens of race and, and instead, advocate for a laser focus on our sense of obligation to one another and our democracy. The physical makeup of our nation is changing; it is beyond time to implore the citizens of this amazing country to each do their part in breaking down these walls. Browning continues:

There are so many groups that [the 2020 administration] has disparaged and insulted. If they can come together as a coalition and keep it together then [his] opponents can win the next two elections. I think that will be absolutely crucial… What do we do about more inflamed divisions in the country in terms of race, class and gender? These problems are not going to be easy to heal.

While it's important for youth of any race today to galvanize their communities, it's just as crucial to ensure the *right* people are in leadership, for they hold the ability to make the change last. Kendi says, "An antiracist America can only be guaranteed if principled antiracists are in power, and then antiracist policies become the law of the land, and then antiracist ideas become the common sense of the people, and then the antiracist common sense of the people holds those antiracist leaders and policies accountable. And that day is sure to come."

How do we get there sooner than later? We set common goals to denounce—loudly—race-based biases. We have the difficult conversations. We help provide avenues for our adults and children to have easy access to education on the history of race in America, provide a roadmap for what we can do to embrace and learn from our growing multiracial society, demand policy change, and vote. Importantly, we begin teaching our children at a young age about implicit bias and strategies to navigate it.

A *Psychology Today* article stated, "While there's no population threshold that, once reached, will signal the end of racism in America, being around more multiracial people can at least nudge monoracials to start thinking and talking more about what race really means." By thinking and talking about what it means, we are given the nudge to also realize what it doesn't mean. It is not a marker. It is not a divider. It is not even a reality. What is a reality? That I have four wonderful, beautiful, smart, multidimensional, amazing children who deserve—just like all children—to grow up in a world that does not limit their potential or put them in a box. They are America. We are America. We deserve better. And *we* are accountable for creating the change we want to see.

ENDNOTES

1   Radley Balko, "21 more studies showing racial disparities in the criminal justice system," *Washington Post*, https://www.washingtonpost.com/opinions/2019/04/09/more-studies-showing-racial-disparities-criminal-justice-system/.

2   Amina Khan, "Getting killed by police is a leading cause of death for young black men in America," *Los Angeles Times*, https://www.latimes.com/science/story/2019-08-15/police-shootings-are-a-leading-cause-of-death-for-black-men.

3   Perception Institute, "Implicit Bias," https://perception.org/research/implicit-bias/.

4   Jennifer Eberhardt. *Biased: Uncovering the Hidden Prejudice That Shapes What We See, Think, and Do*. New York: Penguin Books, 2019.

5   Adeel Hassan, "Hate-Crime Violence Hits 16-Year High, F.B.I. Reports," *New York Times*, https://www.nytimes.com/2019/11/12/us/hate-crimes-fbi-report.html.

6   Ibid.

7   Jennifer Eberhardt. *Biased: Uncovering the Hidden Prejudice That Shapes What We See, Think, and Do*. New York: Penguin Books, 2019.

8   "The War on Marijuana in Black and White," American Civil Liberties Union, https://www.aclu.org/issues/smart-justice/sentencing-reform/war-marijuana-black-and-white.

9   Eileen Rivers, "Nation's failed weed war turned many into prisoners and others into moguls," *USA Today*, https://www.usatoday.com/in-depth/opinion/lifers/2019/09/04/pot-weed-war-marijuana-prison-life-sentence-lifers/2057276001/.

10 Ibid.

11 Jon Greenberg, "10 Examples That Prove White Privilege Exists in Every Aspect Imaginable," *Yes!* magazine, https://www.yesmagazine.org/social-justice/2017/07/24/10-examples-that-prove-white-privilege-exists-in-every-aspect-imaginable/.

12 Eileen Patten, "Racial, gender wage gaps persist in U.S. despite some progress," Pew Research Center, https://www.pewresearch.org/fact-tank/2016/07/01/racial-gender-wage-gaps-persist-in-u-s-despite-some-progress/.

13 "Examples of Discrimination in Society Today," Khan Academy, https://www.khanacademy.org/test-prep/mcat/individuals-and-society/discrimination/a/examples-of-discrimination-in-society-today.

14 Vanderbilt University, "Exploring Unconscious Bias," https://www.vanderbilt.edu/work-at-vanderbilt/diversitytraining/ucb.php.

15 "Adults in Nebraska: Religious composition of adults in Nebraska," Pew Research Center, https://www.pewforum.org/religious-landscape-study/state/nebraska/.

16 Gabriel Stoutimore, "Does Christian Privilege Really Exist? (In America, It Depends On Your Skin Color)," *Relevant* magazine, https://www.relevantmagazine.com/current/christian-privilege-really-exist-america-depends-skin-color/.

17 Chuck Collins, Dedrick Asante-Muhammed, Josh Hoxie, and Sabrina Terry, "Dreams Deferred: How Enriching the 1 Percent Widens the Racial Wealth Divide," Institute for Policy Studies, https://ips-dc.org/racial-wealth-divide-2019/.

18 The Sentencing Project, "Report of The Sentencing Project to the United Nations Human Rights Committee Regarding Racial Disparities in the United States Criminal Justice System," https://www.sentencingproject.org/publications/shadow-report-to-the-united-nations-human-rights-committee-regarding-racial-disparities-in-the-united-states-criminal-justice-system/.

19 "Omaha, Nebraska (NE) income map, earnings map, and wages data," City-Data.com, http://www.city-data.com/income/income-Omaha-Nebraska.html.

20 Jennifer Eberhardt. *Biased: Uncovering the Hidden Prejudice That Shapes What We See, Think, and Do*. New York: Penguin Books, 2019.

21 Jennifer Latson, "The Biracial Advantage," *Psychology Today*, https://www.psychologytoday.com/us/articles/201905/the-biracial-advantage.

22 Karen Turner and Jessica Machado, "5 things people still get wrong about slavery," *Vox*, https://www.vox.com/identities/2019/8/22/20812883/1619-slavery-project-anniversary.

23 CNN, "AC360 study preview: 'Kids on Race: The Hidden Picture,'" https://www.cnn.com/2012/04/02/tv/ac360-study-preview-kids-on-race-the-hidden-picture/index.html.

24 Kim Parker, Juliana Menasce Horowitz, Rich Morin, and Mark Hugo Lopez, "Multiracial in America: Proud, Diverse and Growing in Numbers," Pew Research Center, https://www.pewsocialtrends.org/2015/06/11/multiracial-in-america/.

25 Alexandros Orphanides, "Why Mixed-Race Americans Will Not Save The Country," *Code Switch: NPR*, https://www.npr.org/sections/codeswitch/2017/03/08/519010491/why-mixed-race-americans-will-not-save-the-country.

26 Anekwe, Obiora. 2014. "Global Colorism: An Ethical Issue and Challenge in Bioethics." *Voices in Bioethics* 1 (September). https://doi.org/10.7916/vib.v1i.64

27 National Conference for Community and Justice, "Colorism," https://www.nccj.org/colorism-0.

28 Anekwe, Obiora. 2014. "Global Colorism: An Ethical Issue and Challenge in Bioethics." *Voices in Bioethics* 1 (September). https://doi.org/10.7916/vib.v1i.64

29 Zetta Elliott, "How Do We Share Space?: Black Women Confronting Colorism," *Medium*, https://medium.com/@zettaelliott/how-do-we-share-space-black-women-confronting-colorism-a9ccec1ccd00.

30 Jamelle Bouie and Rebecca Onion, "Slavery Myths Debunked," *Slate*, https://slate.com/news-and-politics/2015/09/slavery-myths-seven-lies-half-truths-and-irrelevancies-people-trot-out-about-slavery-debunked.html.

31 Ibram X. Kendi. *Stamped from the Beginning: The Definitive History of Racist Ideas in America*. New York: Bold Type Books, 2017.

32 Shannon Luders-Manuel, "BlacKkKlansman in Context," *JSTOR Daily*, https://daily.jstor.org/blackkklansman-in-context/.

33 Ibid.

34 Stephen G. Bloom, "Lesson of a Lifetime," *Smithsonian Magazine*, https://www.smithsonianmag.com/science-nature/lesson-of-a-lifetime-72754306/.

35 Aamer Madhani, "Cubs ownership faces backlash after patriarch's racist, Islamophobic emails leaked," *USA Today*, https://www.usatoday.com/story/sports/2019/02/05/cubs-joe-ricketts-racists-emails-islamophobic-backlash/2782712002/.

36 Jennifer Latson, "The Biracial Advantage," *Psychology Today*, https://www.psychologytoday.com/us/articles/201905/the-biracial-advantage.

37 Ibram X. Kendi, *How to Be an Antiracist*. New York: One World; First Edition, 2019.

38 Jennifer Eberhardt. *Biased: Uncovering the Hidden Prejudice That Shapes What We See, Think, and Do*. New York: Penguin Books, 2019.

ACKNOWLEDGMENTS

A short novella intended to document the life and death of my mother and the many beautiful gifts and signs she has bestowed on me since her passing evolved over years into my first book, and I have so many people to thank.

Kathy Hamburger, I will always remember our phone call and you encouraging me to document our story.

Kelly Marie Chavez Coleman, you were with me through my most trying times, and whenever I am in doubt, I hear your words: "Stay strong." We are family, and I am so happy our sons, Q and D, will be forever bonded by the memories of their early years together.

Kris Steed, my soul sister, I would not have met my husband if not for you. Thank you is not enough.

My appreciation to Preston Love, Jr. for sharing his valuable time to school me on civics and set in motion a commitment on my part to be more intentional and engaged in what is happening in our community. You are an inspiring role model of living a purposeful life.

Thank you Chryssa Zizos. Sometimes people have no idea how they are influencing others; you have influenced me more than you know. I can honestly say this would not have happened without your feedback on the novella and pointing me in the right direction. Your words have resonated with me throughout this entire process.

"We cannot function in a multicultural world with mono-cultural mindsets. And, we cannot practice equity and inclusion without cultural competence and system thinking." —Dr. Ramón A. Pastrano IV- MSM, MATS. Ramón, we are excited to see the work you are doing with ImpactLives, Inc. and grateful for you and our Briar Cliff brothers for sharing your cultures and influencing our desire to expand our thinking.

To my courageous friend Shannon Luders-Manuel, I have learned so much from you and can't wait to see your memoir in print and on screen. Thank you for your contributions to *Mixed*, and for helping me understand my privilege and the unique experiences of the biracial community.

I could not ask for a better family; simply put, I grew up surrounded by unconditional love. Dad, Tom, Anne, Lou, Steve, Katy, Julie, I love you all. Aunt J. and Aunt Marilyn, you have helped fill the void of our mother's passing. She sends her appreciation, and so do we.

Finally, to my husband and children: Keith, Quincy, Kaydon, Ezley, and Xonya. I have always had your unwavering support. There are just no words that can express how much I cherish being your wife and mother, or how fortunate I am to have you to love.

ABOUT THE AUTHOR

 Jeanne Jones is a mother, wife, daughter, sister, and author. One of seven children growing up in a predominantly white Midwest city, she had the unique opportunity of being introduced at an early age to people of different races, cultures, and religions. In her adult life she has consistently craved a deeper understanding of how and why racism and indisputable socioeconomic gaps have continued to prevail in America. After becoming the wife of a black man and the mother to biracial and black children, her privilege was amplified in an unexpected way, and her desire to educate herself on these topics grew.

Jones received a Bachelor of Science in Criminal Justice from the University of Nebraska Omaha, where she studied racial disparities in the criminal justice system. She went on to earn a Master of Arts in Liberal Studies from North Central College in Naperville, Illinois, and has completed the Transformational Leadership program through Bellevue University in Omaha, Nebraska. She holds the national certification Certified Manager of Quality / Organizational Excellence through the American Society of Quality, served on the board of directors of the Society of Consumer Affairs Professionals, and spent two decades working for Fortune 500 companies in leadership roles. Her most important role is being a mother, and her dream for her mixed family is to improve race relations in our divided country, one uncomfortable but necessary conversation at a time.